Praise for *Selma and the Liuzzo Murder*

"Jim Turner recounts the true story of how a team of skilled federal lawyers accomplished the seemingly impossible—convicting the klansmen who murdered Viola Liuzzo in 1965—a victory for honest, non-partisan civil rights enforcement that ended a hundred years of klan immunity to the sting of justice."
>   —Roy Reed, *New York Times* reporter who covered Selma and
>   the Liuzzo trials

"The thorough, evidence-based approach that Jim Turner describes was key to securing justice in the South fifty years ago, and it is just as important today as we craft nationwide policies to combat the persistent impact of racial prejudice and discrimination."
—Sarah Rosen Wartell, President, The Urban Institute

"Jim Turner shows us how critical an actively independent Civil Rights Division was to ending Jim Crow. If you have any interest in civil rights history and our policies today—and who doesn't—you have to read this book."
>   —Stanley Pottinger, former Assistant Attorney General for Civil Rights
>   and author of *New York Times* best-seller *The Fourth Procedure*

"All people of good will, regardless of their party preference, can learn from Jim Turner's inspiring story of one of the first civil rights victories. His courageous action is still needed today. Through dedication, perseverance and honest law-enforcement we can protect the basic civil rights of all Americans."
>   —John Dunne, former Assistant Attorney General for Civil Rights,
>   1990–92

"James P. Turner's compelling picture of state prosecutions marred by local prejudice and the successful federal prosecution in this landmark case is a timely reminder of why we need a strong Civil Rights Division in the U.S. Department of Justice when state law enforcement fails to protect our rights."
>   —Brian K. Landsberg, McGeorge School of Law

"We need more Jim Turners in government today."
— Ari Berman, author of *Give Us the Ballot*

"Jim Turner has written a wonderful book. He gives us an insider's view of one of the most important civil rights cases of the 1960s. Forget Grisham and Turow. This is the real deal."
— Gary May, University of Delaware, Author of *The Informant: The FBI, the Ku Klux Klan and the Murder of Viola Liuzzo* and *Bending Toward Justice: The Voting Rights Act and the Transformation of American Democracy*

"Jim Turner's account of finally ending klan terror in the south calls each of us to recommit ourselves to do all we can to finish the work begun at Selma. There's still work left to be done. Get out there and push and pull, until we redeem the soul of America."
— Congressman John Lewis, who led the 1965 Selma to Montgomery Freedom Marches

"Jim Turner knows we will succeed because, in this country, basic human rights for all is our shared heritage. His first case was the 1965 conviction of the Alabama klan killers of Viola Liuzzo, an innocent Detroit housewife who came to help Selma's blacks with few champions. That same year as a young white lawyer raised in Alabama cotton fields where blacks were treated like slaves, I decided to also do civil rights work. *Selma and the Liuzzo Murder Trials* is a civil rights legacy for all who should know our history."
— Morris Dees, Founder, The Southern Poverty Law Center

"Fifty years ago, American justice triumphed over the Alabama klan— thanks to the fearless work of the Civil Rights Division. Jim Turner's moving account reminds us that we can overcome the darkest attacks on human freedom, a lesson well worth remembering today as we confront new challenges to our basic civil rights."
— Deval Patrick, former Governor of Massachusetts and former Assistant Attorney General for Civil Rights

Selma and the Liuzzo Murder Trials

THE FIRST MODERN
CIVIL RIGHTS CONVICTIONS

By James P. Turner

University of Michigan Press
Ann Arbor

Copyright © 2018 by James P. Turner

Published in the United States of America by the
University of Michigan Press
Manufactured in the United States of America
♾ Printed on acid-free paper

2021   2020   2019   2018   4   3   2   1

A CIP catalog record for this book is available from the British Library.
ISBN 978-0-472-07374-0 (hardcover : alk. paper)
ISBN 978-0-472-05374-2 (paper : alk. paper)
ISBN 978-0-472-12353-7 (e-book)

To the committed men and women of the Department of Justice Civil Rights Division, who spent the last fifty-five years building a permanent Constitutional law enforcement program. This program uses federal civil suits and criminal prosecutions to enforce laws that prohibit discrimination on the basis of race, national origin, gender, age, sexual preference, or disability in voting rights, schools, employment, housing, and public accommodations.

It was an honor for me to work with them.

CONTENTS

FOREWORD

by Ari Berman

I first contacted Jim Turner in January 2014 when I was researching my book *Give Us the Ballot* about the history of the Voting Rights Act. He told me he had some documents in his basement I was welcome to come look at.

I took a train to Washington, DC, and drove out to Jim's home in Maryland, which felt like a million miles from the Beltway. It had just snowed and I nearly skidded off the driveway and hit a tree trying to find his secluded house in the woods.

When I arrived, Jim took me down to the basement, which housed thousands of pages of documents spanning his three decades in the Justice Department's Civil Rights Division, organized neatly by year and subject matter. It was a historical gold mine. The archives—now housed at the University of Michigan—were a testament to how much occurred during that time and Jim's pivotal role in helping to shape those events.

If the Civil Rights Division is known as the "crown jewel" of the Justice Department, then Jim was one of its diamonds. He's one of the unsung heroes of the civil rights revolution.

To say that Jim joined the Civil Rights Division at a pivotal moment in American history would be a massive understatement. His first day on the job was February 22, 1965. Just four days earlier, Alabama state troopers had shot a twenty-five-year-old unarmed black man named Jimmie Lee Jackson during a rare night march in Marion, Alabama. Historian Taylor Branch called Jackson the "first martyr of the current campaign for the vote."

At a mass meeting in Selma, the next county over from Marion, James Bevel of the Southern Christian Leadership Conference suggested the idea of marching from Selma to Montgomery to protest Jackson's death. Jackson, a woodcutter and the youngest deacon at his church, had tried unsuccessfully to register to vote five times in Perry County, where only 265 of 5,202 eligible black voters were on the voting rolls. "Jimmie Jackson just wanted to vote," Martin Luther King Jr. said at his funeral. "Now we must see that Jimmie Jackson didn't die in vain."

The march following Jackson's death became known as Bloody Sunday, when Alabama State Troopers brutally beat 800 civil rights marchers, led by John Lewis. The atrocities from Selma, broadcast that evening when ABC interrupted the prime-time premiere of *Judgment at Nuremberg*, shook the nation like no other event in civil rights history. Thousands came to Selma in solidarity. One of them was Jim Reeb, a Unitarian minister from Boston. After a second attempted march from Selma to Montgomery two days later, Reeb took a wrong turn home from dinner and was attacked by white supremacists. He became the second martyr of the Selma campaign for voting rights.

Viola Liuzzo, a mother of five from Detroit, watched history unfold in Selma and knew she had to be there to help. She participated in the triumphant final march from Selma to Montgomery, when 25,000 civil rights activists finally made it to the state capitol. But at the moment of greatest triumph, tragedy struck again, when Liuzzo's car was shot up by klansmen as she returned home from the march. She was the third martyr of the Selma struggle.

For his first major assignment at the Civil Rights Division, Jim was put in charge of overseeing the Liuzzo trial. Seeking justice for the perpetrators of the murder was no easy task at the time. The trial took place in Lowndes County, next to Selma, where not a single African American was registered to vote in March 1965. The case should have been a slam dunk—an undercover FBI informant posing as a klansman testified how he'd witnessed the shooting firsthand. Yet the klan was a badge of pride in places like Lowndes County; the imperial wizard of the united klans of America was the first witness called by the defense.

On May 21, 1965, the all-white jury deadlocked, resulting in a hung jury for klansman Collie Leroy Wilkins, who fired the first shots. A second trial took place in September 1965, a month and a half after President Lyndon

Johnson signed the Voting Rights Act. "The jury deliberated a total of ninety minutes before returning an acquittal" for Wilkins, Turner writes. It wasn't until the Justice Department took over the case—and the trial was moved to the courtroom of Judge Frank Johnson of Montgomery, who authorized the Selma to Montgomery march—that all three klansmen were convicted of a federal conspiracy. It was the "very first modern conviction in a klan assassination ever by a southern jury," Turner writes.

Jim's book is full of vivid details. President Johnson's voice was "quivering with anger" when he announced Liuzzo's murder, he writes. At the Department of Justice compound in Montgomery "the red phone was to the Pentagon; the white one to the White House." When he first got to Alabama, Jim drove the same route as Liuzzo, from Montgomery to Selma, "at frightful speed."

The klan convictions showed how the South was changing, that because of the Voting Rights Act and the work of the Civil Rights Division, the vestiges of Jim Crow were beginning to disappear. Yet it's difficult to read Turner's book today and not wonder whether the arc of history is still bending toward justice, as Martin Luther King famously said.

Unarmed black men have been killed across the country in recent years—in deaths reminiscent of Jimmie Lee Jackson—and the police officers that killed them have not been convicted of the crimes. The Attorney General of the United States is now Jeff Sessions, a product of segregationist Alabama, who twenty years after the passage of the Voting Rights Act shockingly prosecuted civil rights activists from Marion, Alabama, for voter fraud, including Albert Turner, who marched next to John Lewis on Bloody Sunday (they were acquitted). Under Donald Trump, the priorities of the Civil Rights Division are very different from what they were under LBJ.

Jim worked in nine presidential administrations and served under seventeen Attorneys General. He called his first case the most important one he ever worked on. His commitment to justice never wavered—I love the image of him returning to Selma for the fiftieth anniversary of the Bloody Sunday march in 2015. We need more Jim Turners in government today.

PROLOGUE

I joined the Justice Department's Civil Rights Division as a trial lawyer about two weeks before Selma's Bloody Sunday, March 7, 1965, when Alabama police beat and gassed John Lewis and several hundred other voting rights demonstrators back to their churches. Their "crime" was to try to march to Montgomery to ask Governor George Wallace to redress their perpetual grievance of never getting to vote because of their black race. The televised events on this single day would change millions of Americans' views on civil rights, and Bloody Sunday would lead Congress to pass the Voting Rights Act, the Civil Rights Movement's most powerful achievement.

I was one of those who had become committed to using federal authority to stop such discriminatory misconduct anywhere in our country. The Civil Rights Division, established during the Eisenhower administration by the Civil Rights Act of 1957, was where that could be accomplished.[1] In February 1965, the Division hired a batch of young attorneys to help enforce the Civil Rights Act of 1964, which had greatly expanded the law to allow civil

---

1   Introduced in the same year that federal troops had to provide security during desegregation of the Little Rock, Arkansas, schools, the original legislation was designed to provide the Department of Justice with a regular role in future efforts to enforce black civil rights. But after a long debate and a southern filibuster (Senator Strom Thurmond of South Carolina established a single-person record by holding the floor for over twenty-four hours), Congress produced only a toothless substantive compromise, which gave the Attorney General minimal statutory authority to seek federal court orders to allow black people to participate in elections. But as passed, that law also established in the Justice Department a new trailblazing component, the Civil Rights Division, headed by a presidentially appointed and Senate-confirmed Assistant Attorney General.

litigation in federal court to end school segregation and discrimination in public accommodations, employment, and federal programs.

But on criminal matters, the Division had limited prosecuting tools—the only provisions of the federal criminal code that protected civil rights were 18 USC §§ 241 and 242, Civil War Reconstruction Era "anti-klan" laws that had survived and were still on the books. Conviction under these laws could result in up to ten years in jail for conspiracy or one year for defendants who deprived someone of federal rights while acting under "color of law."[2]

In March 1965, Assistant Attorney General John Doar gave me my first mission in Alabama. This book tells the story of how that first assignment became a "shot with a square needle"—an old expression once used to describe the singular loyalty of U.S. Marines where I had also served before attending law school. I stayed in the Division for almost thirty years. When I retired in May 1994, I had spent twenty-five years as its career, that is, non-political, Deputy Assistant Attorney General. In total, I worked in nine national administrations, from Dwight Eisenhower to Bill Clinton, under seventeen consecutive Attorneys General, and as the deputy to seven Assistant Attorneys General for Civil Rights (see James P. Turner, "Used and Abused: The Civil Rights Division," *Washington Post*, December 14, 1997, C1)[3]

---

2   Today, the Division's original staff of fifteen attorneys in 1957 has mushroomed. Supported by the FBI and U.S. attorneys across the country, some 450 lawyers and over 300 other staffers enforce a full spectrum of federal civil rights statutes reaching far beyond racial discrimination. These include discrimination on the basis of national origin, sex, rights of the lesbian, gay, bisexual, transgender, and queer (LGBTQ) community, employment discrimination, Fair Housing Act violations, disability rights, voting rights, school discrimination, police agencies engaged in a pattern or practice of discrimination, and criminal prosecutions under amended 18 USC §§ 241 and 242 and various other criminal laws. This spectacular growth shows that this nation's firm commitment to civil rights was not just some passing fancy.

3   The details are collected in an autobiography, *The Other Side of the Mountain* (Baltimore: Chronicle Press, 2008), available as a Kindle book on Amazon.com. It also describes four oral arguments for the government in the U.S. Supreme Court; and being a Deputy for seven Assistant Attorneys General from both parties: Jerris Leonard (R), David L. Norman (R), J. Stanley Pottinger (R), Drew S. Days III (D), William Bradford Reynolds (R), John R. Dunne (R), and Deval Patrick (D). The author was also nominated for a Senior Executive Service distinguished service award by Democratic President Jimmy Carter, which was presented by Republican President Ronald Reagan.

This book describes the story of the klan murder of Viola Liuzzo at the end of the final Selma to Montgomery march. As you read it, please note that I am fully acquainted with the rules of grammar and understand that words and phrases such as "klan," "klansmen," "grand dragon," "klonsel," and the like are frequently capitalized as if they were honorific titles. But not in this book—these are not honorable titles and will be treated here only as ordinary words identifying common criminals.

While Lyndon Johnson would use Bloody Sunday to get Congress to pass the Voting Rights Act, and Judge Frank Johnson would use it to authorize and protect Dr. King's peaceful march to Montgomery, the federal Liuzzo prosecution would become that very first modern conviction in a klan assassination **ever** by a southern jury.

But, similar to many other stories, this one also had a threatening downside. In 1969, Richard Nixon took office and began implementing his southern strategy, that is, an approach to persuade the white Democrats of the old "Solid South" to switch parties and become Republicans. To do so, he offered to interrupt pending U.S. Supreme Court proceedings by suggesting that the Court "rethink" the need to desegregate with no further delay the all-white schools found unconstitutional in 1954. Division line lawyers immediately petitioned the new Attorney General, John Mitchell, not to do this.

The newly installed Assistant Attorney General for Civil Rights, Jerris Leonard, finally worked out a deal—he would file a petition to the Supreme Court for more time "to think," but he would also promise to accept and to execute whatever that Court ruled. In addition, the Division would be reorganized by subject matter, giving each lawyer a choice of whether to work on school desegregation cases. And finally, to show the new administration's confidence in its career lawyers, two of them (including the author) would be appointed to serve as Leonard's Deputies. In a single week, and with no dissent, the Supreme Court rejected Nixon's "rethinking plan," and the Division went on to desegregate all southern public schools. While Leonard's actions may have saved the Division and given me a long-term job, the Supreme Court filings were also a clear signal that the Republican welcome mat was now open to southerners who supported segregation. Gradually, though Nixon is long discredited and gone, the new South has become solid Republican.

Nixon's successor, President Gerald Ford, was a bit more moderate on civil rights, and even failed to execute effectively Nixon's southern strategy when running against a native southerner, Jimmy Carter. But soon, the reconstituted Republicans would bounce back under Presidents Ronald Reagan and George H. W. Bush. Political fights began to attack minority rights, using code words like "busing" and "quotas" and the need to update and "improve" the Voting Rights Act. The art of the gerrymander was now computerized and regularly used to generate a few more black-controlled districts, while electing many more Republicans.

Today, Republicans control both houses of Congress. Under our first black president ever, the Republicans changed into the party of "no," standing ready to block everything. Their obstruction extended to the Supreme Court itself, culminating in the Senate's nearly yearlong refusal to perform its constitutional duty to consider and vote on a very moderate nominee for the vacancy created by the death of Justice Antonin Scalia.

In short, as hard as it might be to contemplate, one is forced to conclude that the Republican Party founded by Abraham Lincoln has abandoned civil rights. Its recently elected President, Donald Trump, a billionaire who was sued by the Division for violating fair housing laws by discriminating against blacks, now seems aimed at ending our second era of Reconstruction.

Of course, our own experience teaches that there are frequently ways and means to get things done in this country. Just fifty years ago, we started to crawl out of one of our history's deepest holes. We combined the careful rulings of a full and strong Supreme Court with faithful use of bipartisan congressional understandings and the uniform and aggressive, but nonpartisan, enforcement of the nation's civil rights laws. This combination has a name, the solemn promise carved on our Supreme Court building—"Equal Justice Under Law." This is one legacy from Selma that we need urgently to restore today.

SELMA AND THE LIUZZO MURDER TRIALS

Chapter 1

THE CRUSADE AT SELMA

We had come to petition Governor Wallace. We had come to represent the Negro citizens of Alabama and freedom loving people from all over the United States and the world. We had come not only five days and fifty miles, but we had come from three centuries of suffering and hardship. We had come to declare that we must have our Freedom Now. We must have the Right to Vote; we must have equal protection of the law and an end to police brutality.

—DR. MARTIN LUTHER KING, JR.,
"AN OPEN LETTER TO THE AMERICAN PEOPLE"

This is a true story. It took place in central Alabama in 1965, a full century after that fabled Day of Jubilee when slavery was to be ended and replaced by true racial justice. Reconstruction's failure and the South's adoption of Jim Crow showed beyond doubt that new federal statutes would be essential to obtain and deliver black civil rights. In 1964 Congress passed a new Civil Rights Act. Civil rights organizations could now point to the rule of law as the best way out of the country's divisive racial problem, and they could look to the Civil Rights Division of the Justice Department as an enforcement partner. In 1965, that approach was just being put to the test across the South.

When spring came to Alabama that year, one part of the drama played out on the streets of Selma where civil rights groups conducted daily voting rights demonstrations at the Dallas County courthouse. Blacks respectfully asserted their due as citizens, their right as Americans to register and participate as full citizens in the country's electoral process. Millions of Americans watched in disgust, and with a kind of a morbid fascination, at the creative ways Sheriff Jim Clark and the Dallas County Board of Registrars found to frustrate that simple democratic dream. United States District Judge Frank Johnson would later describe the state's reaction as "an almost continuous pattern . . . of harassment, intimidation, coercion, threatening conduct, and sometimes brutal mistreatment."[1]

The pattern in Selma generally followed the practices across the South. Local voting officials resisted at each step on the path to voting, raising every imaginable procedural barrier to allowing blacks to register—from changing the hours of registration, to devising complicated tests for blacks (but none for whites) to pass, to treating black applicants with open hostility, and even to sometimes using the threat of arrests for loitering or disturbing the peace.

And the results were always the same. Without exception white applicants, literate or not, would find their way onto the registration rolls. But no matter what their level of education, almost all blacks—whether decorated veterans, school teachers, or field hands—were failed. For generations, local officials in the South had simply used and abused their authority in order to minimize black participation in the political process.

Eight days after Bloody Sunday, on March 15, 1965, in the greatest speech he ever gave, President Lyndon Johnson of Texas addressed a joint session of Congress on the subject of voting rights. He demanded that the legislators consider and pass the Voting Rights Act he was submitting to end forever all intransigent opposition to the right of black people to register and vote. He spelled out exactly how court records in dozens of cases brought by the Civil Rights Division had demonstrated the denial of the vote to blacks, and how the police in Alabama had beaten marchers just trying to go to Montgomery to seek redress. He concluded we have no "Negro problem," no "Southern problem," no "Northern problem," but there is "only an American problem." And, he ended that speech by solemnly adopting as his own the sacred promise of the movement's civil rights hymn: "We shall overcome"

---

1   Williams v. Wallace, 240 F. Supp. 100, 104 (M.D. Ala. 1965). Judge Johnson noted that in the last three months of a registration drive in Selma, the board of registrars rejected over 78 percent of black applicants. In December 1964, all fourteen black applicants were rejected. In January 1965, 100 of 112 were rejected. In February 1965, 59 of 95 were rejected.

("Transcript of the Johnson Address on Voting Rights to Joint Session of Congress," *New York Times*, March 16, 1965, 30).

Before the summer of 1965 was over, an inspired Congress quickly cut off a southern filibuster, defeated all weakening amendments, and passed the Voting Rights Act of 1965. It is the most effective civil rights legislation ever passed. It authorized federal registration when it was needed and gave authority for federal observers to attend elections designated by the Attorney General. It also required certain "covered jurisdictions" to seek preclearance of every new election related law, and directed the Attorney General to seek court orders ending poll taxes immediately. Enforcement began on the day after it was signed, as federal registrars opened offices in several dozen southern counties over just six months' time.[2]

In short, it was exactly what the blunt-spoken president had ordered: "[T]he goddamnest toughest voting rights act that you can write."[3] One of the major goals of the Civil Rights Movement was reached virtually overnight.[4]

---

2   As Brian K. Landsberg explains, "The Voting Rights Act of 1965 uses a wide menu of innovative techniques to secure the right to vote free from racial discrimination. The act radically changed the enforcement of the Fifteenth Amendment by relying less on the local federal courts and more on the Department of Justice, thus shifting the burden of justification away from those representing blacks and onto voting officials." Landsberg, *Free at Last to Vote: The Alabama Origins of the 1965 Voting Rights Act* (Lawrence: University Press of Kansas, 2007), 3 [notes omitted]. See also Landsberg, *Enforcing Civil Rights: Race Discrimination and the Department of Justice* (Lawrence: University Press of Kansas, 1997).

3   Louis Menand, "The Color of Law: Voting Rights and the Southern Way of Life," *New Yorker*, July 8, 2013.

4   It is worth noting briefly, that in 2013, the United States Supreme Court, by a 5–4 vote, held that the selection system for jurisdictions required to submit voting changes for preclearance was outdated and therefore unconstitutional. This had been the most effective check on backsliding legislation by the worst jurisdictions and had been extended by Congress in a 2006 vote of landslide proportions. In Shelby County v. Holder, 570 U.S. 2 (2013), the majority opinion was written by Chief Justice John Roberts who had been highly critical of preclearance standards while in the Reagan administration Justice Department. After the death of Justice Antonin Scalia and the Senate's refusal to consider any new appointee, the Court had only eight members, and a full court had to wait for the 2016 presidential election. Although Congress has expressed some desire to consider redoing the preclearance formula, many observers doubt that will be done. See, generally, the excellent analysis by Ari Berman, *Give Us the Ballot* (New York: Farrar, Straus and Giroux, 2015).

The record was also clear that the selective enforcement of discriminatory state laws was only one of the engines of segregation. There was another, darker, and more primitive practice also used to keep black people "in their place." The ku klux klan had been a part of Southern life and lore since Reconstruction in the late nineteenth century. Whenever local laws and customs proved inadequate for controlling blacks, masked klansmen astride horses and wearing white robes rode out of the darkness to terrorize, intimidate, and kill.

Part of the klan's mystique was the fact that klansmen would almost never be held accountable for their violent terrorist crimes.[5] Sometimes, sympathetic local lawmen simply looked the other way and declined to file charges. But, even when criminal charges were actually filed, it was the custom, part of the unwritten "Code of the South," that at least one white juror would always find a reason not to convict a local klansmen. In short, the klan had become an active conspiracy of domestic terrorists who murdered, assaulted, committed arson, and bombed to continue fighting the Civil War a full century after its end.

---

5   The klan has been a violent right-wing force in American life since it was formed in Pulaski, Tennessee, in 1865, and then expanded across the South as an antiblack organization (Susan Campbell Bartoletti, *They Called Themselves the KKK: The Birth of an American Terrorist Group* [New York: Houghton Mifflin, 2010], 13–14, 24–26). In 1867, a new klan national leader or "grand wizard" was named, former Confederate General Nathan Bedford Forest, "who, after his victory at Fort Pillow, had summarily executed all black Union soldiers" (Wyn Craig Wade, *The Fiery Cross: The Ku Klux Klan in America* [New York: Simon and Shuster, 1987], 16, 40–41). In 1870–71 Congress passed the Enforcement Act aimed at using federal criminal law to suppress the klan's violent interference with Reconstruction (Wade, *Fiery Cross*, 82–84). But when Jim Crow replaced Reconstruction in 1877, the klan subsided into the background (Bartoletti, *They Called Themselves the KKK*, 71, 74–75). The klan was revitalized in Atlanta in 1915, now focusing on prohibition of alcohol and suppressing Catholics, Jews, and blacks (Wade, *Fiery Cross*, 163–66). It grew quickly in the Midwest and West and by the mid-1920s claimed four to five million members. But it faded again by 1930 to about thirty thousand members. Recent research has documented "4,075 racial terror lynchings in twelve Southern states between the end of Reconstruction in 1877 and 1950" (Equal Justice Initiative, *Lynching in America: Confronting the Legacy of Racial Terror* [Montgomery, Alabama, 2015], 4–6). The klan again revived in the 1950s and 1960s, this time to offer violent opposition to the modern civil rights movement (see Wade, *Fiery Cross*, 302–6).

While much of America raptly followed the Selma demonstrations with growing concern, the members of the Alabama ku klux klan were also watching, but in their case with growing alarm. They worried that the momentum of the civil rights movement might actually change their revered southern way of life. With national attention focused on Selma, they reasoned that this would be the ideal time to, in the words of Alabama governor George Wallace, "send 'em a message"—the South was not going to be pushed around by outside agitators. Klansmen planned and carried out a violent, terrorist attack near Selma, and when they were caught red-handed, they proudly and brashly bragged that no Alabama jury would ever convict them.

The human side of this drama began on March 7, 1965, Selma's Bloody Sunday. Along with millions of other Americans, Viola Liuzzo, a forty-three-year-old mother of five who lived in Detroit, was watching the evening news on her television. Her reaction was typical. She gasped at the graphic clips of Alabama lawmen in gas masks clubbing and gassing peaceful voting rights demonstrators stopped by local police just outside Selma. They intended to march fifty miles to Montgomery to petition George Wallace, the only Governor they had, to redress their grievance that Dallas County officials in Selma would not let them register to vote.[6]

Mrs. Liuzzo rarely participated in political causes, but she soon became captivated by this horrible story. She began to consider the repeated pleas for "people of conscience" to come to Selma in order to participate personally in a new and real voting rights march to Montgomery. When she read that a federal judge had approved a new march, she finally told her husband and family that she had to drive her car to Selma to volunteer her help. As she would explain to friends and family, "This is something I must do" ("Mrs. Liuzzo Felt She 'Had to Help,'" *New York Times*, March 27, 1965, 10).

This simple act of conscience cost Viola Liuzzo her life. She was gunned down by klansmen on March 25, the final day of the march while she and Leroy Moton, a young black man from Selma who worked with Dr. King's

---

6   See photos 1, 2, and 3.

Southern Christian Leadership Conference (SCLC), were driving to Montgomery to bring another load of tired demonstrators back to Selma (Paul L. Montgomery, "Woman is Shot to Death on Lowndes County Road," *New York Times*, March 26, 1965, 1, 23; Roy Reed, "Witness to Slaying Cites Harassment on Road Earlier," *New York Times*, March 27, 1965, 1, 10).

The case was solved overnight. It turned out that one of the four men in the klan car was a paid informant of the FBI (Ben A. Franklin, "4 Alabama Klansmen Charged," *New York Times*, March 27, 1965, 10; "A Liuzzo Suspect Cleared of Charge," *New York Times*, April 15, 1965, 27; Cabell Phillips, "Undercover Men Guarded by F.B.I.," *New York Times*, April 26, 1965, 25).

His voice quivering with anger in a nationwide televised address the very next day, President Johnson announced that federal agents had arrested the three killer klansmen and charged them with conspiracy to violate Viola Liuzzo's civil rights. The president minced no words: "She was murdered by the enemies of justice who for decades have used the rope and the gun and the tar and the feathers to terrorize their neighbors. They struck by night as they generally do, for their purpose cannot stand the light of day" ("Transcript of Johnson's Statement on Arrests in Alabama," *New York Times*, March 27, 1965, 11; see also Charles Mohr, "Bids Congress Act: Calls for Inquiry and Plans Bill to Curb 'Hooded Society,'" *New York Times*, March 27, 1965, 1).

A few days later, a federal grand jury in Montgomery indicted the three klansmen for conspiracy to violate Mrs. Liuzzo's civil right to participate in the court-authorized march ("U.S. Jury Indicts 3 Liuzzo Suspects," *New York Times*, April 8, 1965, 31).

But for all the federal government's vigorous action in finding, arresting, and charging the perpetrators, there were serious problems if this assassination was to be treated as a federal conspiracy. First, these kinds of criminal activities were not normally prosecuted as federal cases. Even though an act might violate both state and federal law, the American justice system traditionally looks to the states, not to the federal government in Washington, DC, to prosecute homicides. Moreover, in 1964, just a year before, in two other cases, the murder of three civil rights workers in Mississippi and the assassination of black motorist Lemuel Penn in Georgia, judges in two different federal trial courts had dismissed similar conspiracy indictments for being outside the scope of federal law. Those dismissals were still pending on the federal government's direct appeal to the Supreme Court.[7]

Finally, even if a federal prosecution were successful, there was only a paltry federal penalty—a maximum sentence of ten years—for what amounted to a political murder. And the extra elements required in a federal conspiracy prosecution were awkward to prove and frequently gave reluctant jurors a convenient excuse to avoid conviction.

Shortly after the federal indictment was returned, Alabama's highest legal authorities—Governor Wallace and Attorney General Richmond Flowers—made a pitch to allow the state to proceed first before any trial of the federal conspiracy charges (see Paul L. Montgomery, "Wallace Pledge," *New York Times*, March 27, 1965, 1). Wallace and Flowers proposed to charge the klansmen with first degree murder and to ask for the death penalty. They asked that the federal government give Alabama justice a chance, turn over to the local prosecutor the entire FBI investigation, and provide access to the informant and all the government's forensic and ballistic evidence. They said they wanted a chance to show the country that Alabama had a civilized justice system that was not controlled by a local code, or by the klan or anyone else.[8]

Over strong objections from major civil rights groups, U.S. Attorney General Nicholas Katzenbach finally agreed to allow Alabama to prosecute first. Attorney General Flower's clinching argument was that even if Alabama failed to convict, it would not preclude, and might even benefit, a later federal trial on the conspiracy charges. Under a long-standing rule, the Supreme Court had held that in these circumstances a second separate trial

---

7   The Supreme Court would not decide these cases until after the three Liuzzo trials described here. In 1966, both dismissals were reversed in United States v. Price, 383 U.S. 787 (1966) and United States v. Guest, 383 U.S. 745 (1966).

8   On the day after the murder the FBI reported that Spencer Robb, Senior Resident Agent in Montgomery, had been contacted about the murder by Governor Wallace. He "expressed complete disgust with the 'cowardly act.'" The Bureau reported that Wallace asked that Alabama state authorities "be afforded the results of the FBI's investigation that would support the issuance of a warrant for murder. . . . His request has been referred to the Department of Justice for appropriate consideration."

for violating federal law does not constitute double jeopardy. In the nation's two-tier legal system, if the same act violates both state and federal law, a trial by the other "sovereign" is not double jeopardy.[9] The federal government had nothing to lose, Flowers argued, and, in fact, it might even benefit from closely observing the state's efforts.[10]

This account describes the efforts over the next eight months to bring to justice the killers of Viola Liuzzo, efforts that took place in three trials—two state prosecutions for murder and one federal prosecution for conspiracy.

---

9   See, e.g., United States v. Lanza, 260 U.S. 377 (1920).

10 We would use the same *Lanza* rule twenty-five years later to bring a second prosecution of the California police officers who had been acquitted in a state trial of the videotaped beating of motorist Rodney King (James P. Turner, "Police Accountability in the Federal System," 30 *McGeorge Law Review*, 991–1017 [Spring 1999]).

Chapter 2

DEATH IN THE DARKNESS
A Bird's-Eye View of the Murder

*At the news of still a third murder we were reminded that this was not a march
to a capitol of a civilized nation as was the march on Washington. We had
marched through a swamp of poverty, ignorance, race hatred and sadism. We were
reminded that the only reason that this march was possible was due to the presence
of thousands of federalized troops, marshals and a Federal Court order. We were
reminded that the troops would soon be going home, and that in the days to come
we must renew our attempts to organize the very county in which Mrs. Liuzzo
was murdered. If they will murder a white woman for standing up for the Negroes'
right to vote, what will they do to Negroes who attempt to register and vote?*

—DR. MARTIN LUTHER KING, JR.,

"AN OPEN LETTER TO THE AMERICAN PEOPLE"

There was death in the warm Alabama air in March of 1965. A cowardly,
random, and senseless political execution was about to take place on Route
80. Twisted minds had conceived this as an act of terrorism so dramatic
that it would make the country reverse its national civil rights policy. In a
wild scene out of the post-Reconstruction South, by shooting a defenseless
woman in the head out on a dark and lonely highway, the ku klux klan was
hoping to kill the nation's awakening commitment to racial justice. Instead,
in the actual world, this highly publicized murder would become the final
straw that made the case for federal action inevitable and irreversible.

Taken from my personal observations and the official trial transcripts,[1] here is the grisly tale that FBI informant Gary Thomas Rowe, Mrs. Liuzzo's passenger Leroy Moton, and state and federal law officers would tell over and over. The vehicle of death was a 1962 white over red Chevrolet Impala sport sedan. Its four occupants hailed from Bessemer, a seedy suburb of Birmingham. The driver was Eugene Thomas, a sometime steelworker. Next to him was William Orville Eaton, slight, sickly, an occasional steel worker, then out of work. Behind the driver in the rear seat was Rowe, a burly, rough-and-ready redhead who had bounced from job to job across the South. In the right rear was Collie Leroy Wilkins, at twenty-one the youngest of the group, a self-styled "shade tree mechanic" who fixed cars in his parents' backyard.

All four were members of Bessemer's Eastview klavern (local klan group) of the united klans of America. Decked out in coat and tie for the occasion, they were all dressed up by klan standards. While they knew each other as klansmen, this was their first "mission" together. Except for young Wilkins, each had a wife and family in Bessemer. Except for Wilkins, each carried a gun.

For five years, Tommy Rowe, as he was called, had been serving as a secret paid informant for the FBI. He had received a last-minute phone call that morning from Gene Thomas, the klan enforcer designated to organize and lead this action. Thomas stated that Rowe had been assigned to join a group heading for Montgomery to observe the last leg of the civil rights march. The last-minute call was part of the klan's security system to prevent the plan from being leaked to the FBI. Other than the time and place to meet, Thomas gave no details.

When Rowe inquired about their activity at the march site, Thomas responded with klan small talk about maybe "bustin' heads" or "something." The FBI's standing instruction had been that Rowe should accept such an assignment, but must consult with his contact agent before going.

---

1   The author has donated the files and records gathered during his service in the Justice Department to the University of Michigan Library, where they are available to the public. The official transcripts and other materials relating to the three Liuzzo prosecutions discussed in this book are available online at http://www.press.umich.edu/p/selma.

Rowe immediately called his Bureau contact, Special Agent Neil Shanahan, who told him to go with the group. If possible, he was to check in by phone during the day, but he absolutely must report by phone as soon as he returned. As usual, and with no details about how to honor this order, Shanahan also admonished that Rowe should avoid participating in anything "unlawful." Shanahan then relayed word of Rowe's trip to his supervisor, who in turn notified the Alabama state police that the Thomas car was headed for Montgomery carrying klansmen who were "armed and dangerous."

The ride to Montgomery was uneventful. The four got better acquainted and the car soon became full of the standard klan gossip about the march. They shared tales of the interracial sexual debauchery said to be taking place among the marchers and concluded that the scum from "up North" were nothing but "pot smokers" and "nigger lovers." They should all be run out of the state. Their conversations soon developed a sense of comradeship. They snarled about how someone needed to show that "Martin Luther Coon" that he can't walk all over us. They began to call each other "Bro" for brother; young Wilkins was dubbed the "Baby Bro."

They hung out for a bit in Montgomery watching as a crowd of 25,000 gathered for speeches at the state capitol building. When Thomas announced it was time to leave and head toward Selma, they did so, pausing in the Montgomery outskirts for beer and sandwiches.[2]

About ten miles from Selma, they were stopped at a state police roadblock for a noisy muffler. Klansmen always looked on state troopers as their allies. After all, every Alabama trooper was a white man and the front license plate of every patrol car sported the Confederate stars and bars. For whatever reason, there is no indication that the FBI's warning to Alabama state police headquarters about this very vehicle driven by Eugene Thomas ever reached the officers manning the roadblock outside Selma. Thomas got out of the car, glad-handed the trooper a bit and, never revealing how he did it, somehow persuaded the trooper to let them go with just a warning ticket. It was issued at 6:20 p.m.

---

2 FBI agents later found and interviewed a waitress at the restaurant there who remembered Rowe loudly hustling her.

When they reached Selma, the klansmen stopped at the Silver Moon Cafe, the epicenter of white hostility to the civil rights marchers. Thomas bragged that a couple of weeks before a patron from there had gone outside with a baseball bat and killed "some ol' preacher from Massachusetts" (the Reverend James Reeb was clubbed on a Selma street on March 9, 1965, and later died).[3] As they left, a man Thomas identified as out on bail for killing Reeb advised them: "Well, God bless you boys, go do your job, I have already did mine." With that benediction, the four got in the Chevrolet and began to cruise through Selma to see the sights. There was still no discussion of any specific plan. Later, Rowe would tell prosecutors that he was getting more nervous by the moment.

Local residents advised FBI investigators that Mrs. Liuzzo reported her drive from Detroit to Selma had been uneventful. She arrived about a week before the date set for the new march and was put up with a black family in the "project," the street name for Selma's George Washington Carver public housing development in the neighborhood where the voting rights drive was centered. They also stated that most of her "work" for the demonstration involved the use of her 1964 light blue Oldsmobile hauling people and packages to and from Montgomery. To help her find her way around she was teamed with nineteen-year-old Leroy Moton, who lived in the project and worked for the transportation committee of the Southern Christian Leadership Conference. She usually stayed with her assigned hosts in Selma while Moton used her car for the SCLC transport and delivery work.

The same sources stated that when the march started, Mrs. Liuzzo did not trek the entire fifty miles to the capital, but she did march along as they left Selma and then got a ride to Montgomery to hear the speeches on March 25.[4] She later saw Leroy Moton at St. Jude's, a Catholic school and

---

3   Reverend Reeb and three other ministers were beaten on "Turnaround Tuesday," March 9, 1965, during a second attempt to march past the Edmund Pettis Bridge. The marchers decided to return to Selma to comply with a federal court order. Reeb died two days later. According to press reports, four Selma men were indicted for Reeb's murder. Three were acquitted by all-white juries and the fourth fled to Mississippi. All four have now died. This "cold case" was briefly reopened by the FBI, but no prosecution resulted (Jay Reeves, "Final Suspect in 1965 Civil Rights Slaying Dies in Alabama," Associated Press, September 1, 2016).

4   See photos 4, 5, and 6.

hospital on the edge of Montgomery. They packed her car with an exuberant, racially mixed group of youngsters who needed a ride back to Selma. The car was soon awash with giddy excitement over the day's events—the enormous turnout, Dr. King's wonderful speech, and how they all had sore feet, just like Rosa Parks whose tired feet had started the 1955 Montgomery Bus Boycott. After they dropped their load of young people at Brown Chapel AME (African Methodist Episcopal) Church, the SCLC headquarters in Selma, they were asked to go back to Montgomery to pick up another load of returning marchers. As they passed the bank on the way out of town, Moton noticed the time/temperature sign said 7:34 p.m.

"Hey, Bro, looka there. A white woman drivin' a nigger around in her car," Rowe reported the conversation began. The occupants of the klan Chevrolet immediately perked up. One gushed that they may have found some "important nigger, maybe a leader of the march." Another speculated that the two were probably going somewhere to "make out," and suggested, "Follow them. Maybe we can catch 'em in the act." The driver, Thomas, then began to follow Mrs. Liuzzo's Oldsmobile east on Route 80 toward Montgomery.

Rowe reported that on several occasions Thomas began to pull next to the Oldsmobile to "take 'em," but each time Rowe, still unaware of exactly what was planned, would call attention to some problem to divert him—a jeep load of soldiers, the state police roadblock, oncoming traffic. But although Thomas would drop back momentarily, he did not give up chasing the Oldsmobile, and when the coast was clear he accelerated the pursuit at a high rate of speed.

After the road narrowed to two lanes a few miles east of Selma, without anyone noticing it the two speeding cars passed into Lowndes County. On the March to Montgomery this had been the darkest, scariest stretch of all. Lowndes had a serious history of oppressing black people. Even though blacks outnumbered whites by more than four to one, the blacks there were the poorest of the poor, illiterate sharecroppers whose circumstances had changed very little since the Civil War. In Lowndes, the segregation of the races was absolute. Not a single black person was registered to vote. "Colored schools" were wooden shacks set on cinder blocks with outdoor privies. The county's grim reputation for racial violence had earned it the local nickname of "Bloody Lowndes."

In dark and bloody Lowndes, on March 25, 1965, the two cars raced inexorably toward an epic American tragedy. Moton said that Mrs. Liuzzo was driving along, chatting away, unaware of any danger. Just as the Thomas car pulled alongside as if to pass, Moton said he had leaned forward from the passenger seat to tune in a favorite Nashville station. In the other car, by Rowe's account, Collie Leroy Wilkins, the crew-cut, pudgy twenty-two-year-old high school dropout, with a narrow forehead and close-set eyes, was eager to impress his "bros." Rowe would testify that without a word, and using a pistol Thomas had quietly handed him, Wilkins extended his arm out the right rear window and, point blank, fired two shots into the closed driver's window of the Liuzzo Oldsmobile. Thomas began yelling for everyone to "shoot," and Eaton and Rowe reacted. Before they cleared the Olds, Eaton began to fire and Rowe extended his arm past Wilkins and pretended to fire. Eaton and Wilkins both emptied their guns in the fusillade.[5]

The Olds drifted to the right, angled off the road, traversed the barrow pit (roadside ditch), and crashed into a farmer's fence. Viola Liuzzo was dead. Miraculously, Leroy Moton escaped unscathed. Somehow, the shots had traversed the front seating area without striking him. Investigators later found one bullet that had burrowed into the interior car roof directly above the passenger seat. Bending forward to tune the radio likely saved Moton's life. There was a live eyewitness of this murder in each of the cars.

As the shooters sped back to Bessemer to arrange an alibi, Leroy Moton ran down Route 80 for five miles before he finally flagged down a truckload of returning marchers. At the first opportunity they reported the incident to a state trooper who proceeded to the grisly site. After reporting the murder to the police, Moton would be held in jail overnight under "protective custody" (Roy Reed, "Witness to Slaying Cites Harassment on Road Earlier," *New York Times*, March 27, 1965).[6]

---

5   See photos 7, 8, and 9.

6   Years later, after serving their federal sentences, two of the convicted conspirators ended their silence and claimed that, despite the ballistic evidence introduced at the trial where they were convicted, Rowe had been the first shooter. The Liuzzo family filed a civil action against the federal government seeking damages, and an Alabama Grand Jury indicted Rowe. After a full hearing, Georgia refused to extradite Rowe to Alabama for trial, and the family's civil case was dismissed. See discussion in the epilogue.

Chapter 3

STARTING THE ENGINES
OF JUSTICE IN ALABAMA

*If two or more persons conspire to injure, oppress, threaten or intimidate any
person in any State, Territory or District in the free exercise or enjoyment of any
right or privilege secured to him by the Constitution or laws of the United States,
or because of his having so exercised the same . . . They shall be fined under this
title or imprisoned no more than ten years or both.*

—18 USC § 241

I joined the Justice Department's Civil Rights Division on February 22, 1965,
just about a month before the Liuzzo murder, when the Division was adding additional staff to enforce the wide-ranging Civil Rights Act of 1964.
This new law had been sponsored first by President John F. Kennedy in 1963
and then pushed through Congress by his successor, President Johnson, the
following year as the best way to honor the slain leader's commitment to
racial justice. I was assigned to the section charged with enforcing the new
law in Mississippi and Louisiana, but within two weeks the events in Selma
commanded everyone's attention.

While I watched from Washington, the Department joined a civil lawsuit brought by Hosea Williams, the SCLC's Special Projects Director,
against Alabama Governor George Wallace. After Bloody Sunday, it asked
for a court order that would require the state to permit and protect a new
voting rights march to Montgomery. The First Amendment to the U.S.
Constitution specifically protects "the right of the people peaceably to as-
semble, and to petition the government for a redress of grievances." Here, the

very well-founded grievance was the rigid refusal of Dallas County's voting officials to allow black people the basic right to register and vote.

The federal judge was Frank Johnson, a civil rights legend in Alabama. He quickly issued the order permitting the march and specifying a detailed plan for how it was to be conducted. When Governor Wallace complained that the state government would not be able to protect the demonstrators against local hostility, Judge Johnson ordered the federal government to take over that job by federalizing the Alabama National Guard and, if necessary, by using regular army troops.

But while most new Division lawyers were in Alabama gathering facts and drafting papers for the case or working on the logistics for the march, I had to stay in Washington, reading stale FBI reports about minor incidents in Mississippi. A Marine Corps veteran, I had joined the Division to participate in the nation's long overdue civil rights enforcement effort. But I was now left just sitting on the bench while thousands of people from all over our country poured into Selma to march freedom's message to Montgomery. At least once a day, I called to volunteer to participate. Assistant Attorney General John Doar merely replied that I had to be patient, and accept the assurance that he would be calling on me "soon." I was still sitting and waiting on March 25 when the march reached Montgomery and news of the shocking murder of Viola Liuzzo was relayed to Doar while he was dining at Montgomery's Elite (locally "ee-light") Café.

The next morning Doar called and asked me to please come to Montgomery. Within hours, a U.S. Air Force Jet-Star delivered me to Maxwell Air Force Base and a United States Marshal took me to the command post in the federal post office building. Doar then launched into a detailed, head-spinning briefing about the current situation in Selma and Montgomery and quickly pointed to each of the various communication systems that had been established by the Justice Department for the march. The red phone was to the Pentagon; the white one went to the White House. Another was a hotline to the Department in Washington.

Reacting to yet another killing of a civil rights worker, the SCLC had announced plans to demonstrate at the Alabama state capitol building by delivering coffins representing all those who had been killed in the struggle.

The Student Non-violent Coordinating Committee (SNCC) had planned a memorial service at the site of the Liuzzo killing in Lowndes County. Doar quickly introduced me to U.S. Attorney Ben Hardeman, the ranking U.S. Marshal and the FBI Special Agent in Charge. Abruptly, luggage and raincoats appeared and it began to dawn on me that he and all the other tired and disheveled lawyers were preparing to leave that very moment. Doar made direct eye contact with me, and quietly ordered, "You're in charge here. Go to the coffin demonstration and call me every two hours." Then, he and his whole tired group just walked out.

Had my fortunes changed! In just a few hours, I had gone from the sulky reader of dispatches to being a field commander of the final stages of a major civil rights operation. I even had a small air force—one plane from the Border Patrol—that had been assigned to provide reconnaissance. Pretty heady stuff for a thirty-four-year-old lawyer who a month earlier had been prosecuting DUI cases in Colorado.[1]

Of course, I never got the chance to issue any commands or tell the airplane where to go. Instead, I attended the coffin demonstration, which was very uneventful, and I carefully watched as no one showed up at the planned SNCC memorial service, one of many scheduled demonstrations that never actually happened.

Then, Doar directed me by phone to go to Selma to check with our attorneys there. Thinking about what the klan did to that white lady from Detroit the night before, I asked if he thought I should get the Bureau or a marshal to drive me over. "Don't bother them," he said, "they are probably tired. Just take one of the rental cars and go." My first trip on U.S. Route 80 to Selma was made at a frightful speed, alternatively looking over one shoulder for cars full of night riders and over the other for the klan assassins I knew were lurking behind every tree in Bloody Lowndes.

---

1   While waiting in the FBI office to meet the Special Agent in Charge, I bumped into Roy Reed, an Arkansawyer who had been my college roommate at Missouri University. Both of us had studied journalism, joined the armed forces, and gone to graduate school. We had not seen each other since 1952. He was covering the Selma action for the *New York Times*. We rekindled our dormant friendship on the spot and it has continued to this day.

I arrived without incident, and after a day of learning a bit about Selma, Doar told me to return to Montgomery and get ready to assist one of his deputies, St. John Barrett, who would be presenting the shooting of Mrs. Liuzzo to the federal grand jury. This became the beginning of my total immersion in civil rights law enforcement.

The first thing was to collect the facts. As the investigative branch of the Department, the FBI had already begun to gather the facts needed to support the charge of a conspiracy to violate civil rights. Normally, the Bureau does its work and presents Department lawyers with a final written report, which they use to identify witnesses needed to obtain an indictment. In this case, we were to proceed to the grand jury before the final report was ready, so Barrett and I had to get briefings directly from the investigating agents. Our most graphic briefing was from Special Agent Ed Leahy, who drove us on a reenactment of the klan car's chase. When informant Tommy Rowe's narrative said Thomas was going over 100 miles per hour as he tried to catch the Olds, I watched the speedometer in the Bureau's souped-up Plymouth faithfully register that same speed.

Once in the grand jury, there was no problem getting the necessary twelve votes for the indictment from the total of twenty-three grand jurors. The case was airtight. The testimony of two eyewitnesses was verified in almost every detail by scientific and other evidence. The state police produced the warning ticket that placed the Thomas car on Route 80 shortly before 7:00 p.m. A search warrant for the Eugene Thomas house turned up his gun, and FBI ballistics experts matched the bullet from the victim's head to that weapon. Agents had found shell casings along the highway right where Rowe said they were thrown, and they, too, matched the klan weapons.

While some of the white jurors plainly did not fancy voting for something labeled "civil rights" and there was a little undercurrent that maybe Rowe should have done something to prevent this murder, the Alabama jurors followed the law as the prosecutors explained it and voted to indict the three klansmen for conspiracy.

A couple of weeks later in Washington, Doar met with me and explained that Attorney General Nicholas Katzenbach had agreed with the State of Alabama's request that it be allowed to try state murder charges before the federal civil rights case. It was a little like that first day in Montgomery. Doar made direct eye contact with me and said, "You know this case from the bottom up. I need you to be in charge of providing all the federal evidence to the state. Work with the FBI agents. Get to know the local prosecutors and let me know if you think this is a genuine effort." He then concluded with his standard order, "Call me every day."

Chapter 4

LOWNDES COUNTY
The Spring Term of Court

[One very balanced southern editorial view: Dr. King did it.]

We hold no brief for those who came from the four corners of the country to march in Alabama. This doesn't mean, however, that we give sanction to or applaud attacks and killings. Two wrongs have never made a right and they never will.

The law enforcement agencies of Alabama must leave no stone unturned in their effort to bring to justice the persons responsible for this crime. The courts of that state must, if any sense of law and order is ever to prevail in this nation again, conduct the resultant trial free of any prejudice or bias whatsoever. Alabama must meet this obligation to her sister states of the South.

While deploring the incident itself, we must confer upon Dr. Martin Luther King the prime responsibility for this heinous deed.

—SAVANNAH EVENING PRESS, MARCH 26, 1965

The criminal docket in Lowndes County was not crowded and the local prosecutor, Arthur C. Gamble, called "Bubba" by his friends, told us he wanted to strike while the "iron was hot." He advised us that he actually intended to bring this first-degree murder indictment of the three klansmen to trial during the spring term of the court, which commenced less than six weeks after the crime. He would present the critical witnesses to the Lowndes County Grand Jury, scheduled to meet on April 19, and would begin trying the case during the first week of May. I advised the FBI of this accelerated schedule and promptly flew off to Alabama, anxious to meet this prosecutor-in-a-hurry.

Gamble was an affable, open kind of guy. He stood a little over six feet and spoke softly, but with authority. We never discussed the right to vote or other civil rights issues. His attitude was straightforward, no nonsense, projecting an air of quiet confidence. He asked when he could interview the FBI's informant and the other witnesses under the federal government's control. He said that, insofar as possible, this case would be treated like any other serious homicide. He would personally present the matter to the grand jury assisted by the County Solicitor and someone from the state Attorney General's office. He would schedule meetings with the Alabama officials involved—the Sheriff, the state police, and the state toxicologist—but he did ask for assistance in meeting with Moton and the FBI's paid informant, Tommy Rowe.

Leroy Moton worked for the SCLC's transportation committee, taking SCLC officials and visitors from and to the airport and running other errands. He was not represented by counsel and, after spending a night in jail for just reporting this crime, he had some genuine distrust of local authorities and insisted on not meeting with any city or county officials unless a federal representative was present. While the FBI carefully took its paid informant everywhere, its firm policy precluded using agents for supporting other witnesses. I agreed to meet and go with Moton when he met Gamble. I would see a lot of Moton during all three trials and got to like and respect him. Gamble assured Moton that all he needed was his testimony about being fired upon while in Mrs. Liuzzo's car. He then subpoenaed him before the grand jury for a very short appearance. Gamble was not blown away by Moton, but pronounced that his testimony was "satisfactory."[1]

As for Tommy Rowe, we arranged for the FBI to bring him from a secret location in Florida to Maxwell Air Force Base in Montgomery where he would meet with the prosecutor. I also sat in on that meeting. Rowe was extremely jumpy at the prospect of coming back into Alabama. He was convinced that publicity about his perceived "betrayal" of the klan would make him a target for assassination. Because he believed that Alabama law

---

1   See photo 14.

enforcement officers cooperated with the klan, he did not want to mix with them. He was also extremely jittery in the presence of reporters.

Rowe explained his cautious conduct with police and reporters because in his preceding five years with the klan he had quickly learned from his klan buddies that Alabama police were really their friends. According to Rowe, in 1961 when the freedom riders were to be arrested in Birmingham, he advised the FBI that the local cops had agreed to delay the arrests for fifteen minutes to give local klansmen, including Rowe, a chance to attack the civil rights demonstrators. One of the ruses the klan frequently used, Rowe said, was to get up close to their victims by carrying a pencil and pad, posing as reporters. Rowe complained that he was now being sent into a rural Alabama county, containing a hotbed of klan sympathizers, to blow the whistle publicly on a klan murder while dozens of so called "reporters" milled all around. And he was to do all this while being "protected" by Alabama cops.

Over the next few months, I had an opportunity to get to know Rowe. For an FBI informant, his background was slightly above average. He had dropped out of school in the ninth grade. His physical appearance made him seem a credible klansman. He stood a little under six feet and weighed a little over 200 pounds. He was redheaded, blustery, high strung, a little paunchy, but physically strong. He had bounced from job to job across the South from his native Georgia to Memphis and finally to Birmingham. His dissolving second marriage to a nurse had produced four kids. He drank way too much and, all in all, seemed the ideal type to serve as a klan informant—a rough-cut guy with no special skills—who was committed to helping the Bureau.

Watching him with the FBI agents, I concluded that, deep down, Tommy Rowe really wanted to be a cop. He was very committed to the Bureau and was extremely tight with his managing agent, FBI Special Agent Neil Shanahan. But he also liked the excitement of his dangerous profession. I suspect, but do not know, that while working inside the klan he may have tried to divert suspicion occasionally by straying from the Bureau's regularly repeated Hippocratic admonitions to "do no harm."

Later, I sat in on Gamble's interview with Rowe. Gamble went over the whole story with him and probed him on several details. Both men seemed a bit wary of the other. Rowe was uneasy and defensive whenever Gamble seemed to question his memory or suggest he was embellishing. Gamble's questions related only to the Liuzzo case and did not cover any of Rowe's earlier work for the Bureau. Afterward, Gamble sought my view of Rowe and I told him that the FBI had confidence in the information that he was providing, and urged him to talk to Special Agent Shanahan, who handled Rowe.

Neil Shanahan, one of my all-time favorite agents, was an easy-going Irishman who had formed a tight bond with Rowe. (When Rowe later joined the federal witness protection program, he would choose "Neil" as his middle name.) Shanahan not only convinced Gamble that Rowe could be trusted, but Gamble thought Shanahan was so persuasive that he asked the FBI agent to testify about Rowe before the grand jury.

When a nervous Rowe came to Hayneville to appear before the grand jury, he was provided with a full FBI escort. He rode in the back seat of a bureau car with Shanahan.[2] We anticipated that several dozen reporters would be swarming around the courthouse and knew how their presence would strike fear into Rowe that they were infiltrated by the klan. With the prosecutor, we arranged to get Rowe into the grand jury room by a side door while members of the media were diverted to the front of the courthouse by the arrival of two FBI decoy cars. Several agents jumped out of the decoys and began to push the reporters back as though clearing the way for Rowe. The ruse worked and Rowe made it inside without being noticed or approached by anyone.

But getting him out of the grand jury and back into the FBI car was a horse of a different color. At the appointed time, a half dozen agents, some state police, and I had planned to wedge ourselves into strategic positions in a way that would block media access to the front courthouse breezeway and stay there just long enough for Rowe to hurry out of the building and hustle into an FBI car waiting at the back of the courthouse. And, almost everyone was delayed just long enough for Rowe to make it, but one aggressive report-

---

2   See photo 15.

er, Jack Nelson of the *Los Angeles Times*, somehow managed to squirm right through our line like a crafty National Football League running back. Then, I watched in terror as, in a perfect re-creation of Rowe's doomsday scenario, Nelson ran straight toward him as he was entering the car. Nelson was waving his reporter notebook and calling out loudly, "Mr. Rowe, Mr. Rowe."

As he neared the car, I saw Nelson suddenly stop, raise both hands and begin backing away as the car burned rubber. The outraged reporter later claimed that the FBI informant had been aiming a pistol at him as the car sped away. I later found out (unofficially) that the escorting agents had to forbid Rowe from carrying his personal weapon into the grand jury, but, as a compromise, had promised that he could borrow one of theirs the instant he got back into the Bureau's car. When Nelson's editors raised an official complaint with the FBI that a government informant had tried to shoot one of their reporters, the agency replied that Rowe, who sometimes smoked a pipe, was holding his pipe and a tobacco pouch, which Nelson must have mistaken for a gun. Somehow, no one could ever convince Jack that the pistol he thought he saw was really just a smoking pipe.

After two days of testimony, the Lowndes County grand jury returned first-degree murder indictments against Wilkins, Thomas, and Eaton. This was the state's first major step on the road to justice. Gamble then decided to try the defendants separately, beginning with Wilkins, the first shooter who likely had killed Mrs. Liuzzo.[3] Forensics had confirmed the eyewitness testimony and established beyond a doubt that Wilkins had leaned out of the backseat and fired directly at the victim with the weapon provided by Eugene Thomas. If anyone could be convicted in Alabama, it had to be the "baby bro." The Wilkins trial would begin on May 3, 1965, only thirty-nine days after the killing. This seemed very soon to schedule a major murder trial, but Gamble said that quickly engaging the wheels of justice would be a public expression of his confidence in the case. No delay was sought by the defense.

While the prosecutor seemed somewhat confident of a conviction, this was made very doubtful not only by his haste in scheduling the trial but also

---

3   See photo 16.

by questions about his ability to steer a highly bigoted all-white jury. And the trial would later develop other issues—the FBI had made some mistakes and the trial judge would not control defense counsel at all. In short, even with the testimony from eyewitnesses and the mountain of real and forensic evidence confirming that the defendants had committed the crime, there was precious little ground for any real optimism.

Chapter 5

TRIAL DAY ONE
Selecting the Jury

The right of trial by jury is of ancient origin, characterized as "the glory of the English law" and "the most transcendental privilege which any subject can enjoy."

—DIMICK V. SCHIEDT, 293 U.S. 474, 486 (1934)

A white, male jury was chosen Monday to try a young Alabamian for his life in the slaying of a white woman civil rights demonstrator. A Ku Klux Klan leader sat at the defense table. . . . Women are not eligible for jury duty in Alabama state courts. The only Negro on the panel of prospects asked to be excused because of a work injury.

—ASSOCIATED PRESS, "JURY SELECTED TO HEAR LIUZZO
SLAYING TRIAL," MAY 4, 1965

On the morning of May 3, 1965, in the hamlet of Hayneville—pronounced Hay-knee-ville by many local residents—I was goggle-eyed as the big circus came to town. The town's grassy square was dominated by the courthouse, a gleaming white Greek revival building that had stood there since 1856, five years before secession. The square teemed with people, curious locals mixing with reporters and many other out-of-towners. The general scene called to mind the set for *Inherit the Wind*, that wonderful play about what was labeled the "monkey trial," the 1925 Scopes case over whether it was legal to teach evolution in Tennessee. The scene raised the question of whether this Alabama antebellum courthouse could produce only antebellum justice.[1]

---

1   The courthouse with the Confederate monument in front is shown in photo 10.

Southern Bell had hastily installed a bank of pay phones behind the courthouse for media use. The national press corps was out in full strength, with TV cameras, radio reporters, and dozens of the pencil press, national and international.[2] Alabama lawmen by the dozen, uniformed and every one a white male, were there to maintain order.

Klan loyalists, who normally had few opportunities to get onto a public stage, were all dressed up in jackets and ties for the occasion. They proudly strutted around the square behind imperial wizard Robert Shelton of the united klans of America, who came from his home in Tuscaloosa. Their new celebrities, klansmen Wilkins, Thomas, and Eaton, walked along with the wizard and other high but slightly lesser klan leaders—grand dragons and dragons, and so on. Klansmen Thomas and Eaton were attended by their wives and children, their hyper teenage sons all puffed up, well scrubbed, and chasing attention.

An integrated delegation of civil rights workers from Selma, slightly scruffy in denim and long hair, clustered in one corner of the square, trading contemptuous glances with the parade of klansmen. The square was virtually full. Every white person from the area had found some reason to come to town that morning. Even a few Lowndes County blacks were curious enough to kind of peek in from the outer edges of the square.

Members of the media were especially drawn to defense counsel Matt H. Murphy, Jr., of Birmingham. A tall, curly-headed, rough-cut man in his fifties, he was born in Birmingham and grew up in prosecutor Gamble's hometown of Greenville. Murphy's father had been an outspoken segregationist lawyer who ran unsuccessfully for Alabama Lieutenant Governor in the 1930s. Murphy got his law degree from the University of Alabama in 1948, and claimed a practice that specialized in defending klansmen. He was given—or had assumed—the honorary title of "klan klonsel," the general counsel to Alabama's largest klan faction, the united klans of America.

There to greet supporters and meet the public, the klonsel, wizard, and dragons all walked around the square, stopping here and there to talk to

---

2   Most prominent were Roy Reed of the *New York Times* and Jack Nelson of the *Los Angeles Times*.

reporters and others. In fact, we would learn later that Murphy was actually not a very good lawyer, and hardly anyone could remember him representing clients who were not klan connected. He was missing two fingers on his right hand, lost it was rumored in some kind of klan fracas in his younger days, and he would frequently raise his damaged hand to make the V for victory symbol. He made a flamboyant figure on the square with his curly graying hair, light tan suit, and brown straw hat, waving his maimed hand about and responding to press questions in a loud, gravelly voice. On his lapel Murphy sported a KKK insignia and the "NEVER" button popularized by Selma's Sheriff Jim Clark as the one word answer to the whole Civil Rights Movement.[3]

Klonsel Murphy delivered his message in the center of the square, near the memorial obelisk on which was carved the names of Lowndes County's Civil War Confederate dead—some with the very same surnames of people who had been called for today's jury. His message was simple and timeless: his clients, "these boys," he proudly called them, are "heroes" and "no jury in the State of Alabama will ever convict them."

The parade finally ended when the somber-faced High Sheriff—wearing a cowboy hat and a holstered pistol strapped to his belt—escorted a group of white men across the square and into the courthouse. These were the prospective jurors.[4]

Most of these veniremen (the prospective jurors) had the walk and look of men of the soil. Many tugged at their unfamiliar neckties. Only one black person had been included in their ranks. Plainly, this would be the usual, all white, all male Lowndes County jury.[5] For all his bluster and fierce bravado, Murphy had pointed one of the remaining fingers on his right hand directly at the crucial question in this case: Could the judicial system of a Black Belt Alabama county, developed from the turmoil of the nineteenth century, pro-

---

3   Murphy was featured on the cover of *LIFE Magazine*, May 21, 1965, see photo 13.
4   It would be well into the 1970s before the U.S. Supreme Court discovered that the Constitution required that states must allow women to serve as jurors. When Alabama had to accept its first women jurors under a federal court order in 1966, every other state except Mississippi and South Carolina already allowed women to serve. See White v. Crook, 251 F.Supp. 401 (M.D. Alabama, 1966).
5   No black person had ever served on a Lowndes County jury.

duce twelve white men willing to set aside their inclinations and judge this case on the facts presented in court?

The large second floor courtroom was impressive with high ceilings and tall windows open to the breezes (and to an occasional misguided bird). The elevated judge's bench and jury box occupied the end away from the square. There were oak tables for counsel and a witness chair next to the judge's bench. An oak railing separated the spectators from the participants. Back behind the spectators' section was something I had never seen in a courtroom, before or since. A rear corner of the room was blocked off with steel bars, painted institutional grey, forming a courtroom lockup—a public detention cell for defendants. County officials claimed that it had not been used for years, and was still kept in the courtroom "just for display." [6]

The presence of this cage—shrugged off by slightly embarrassed locals as a leftover from the past—lent an ominous mood to the entire room, a mood that spoke volumes about the nature of southern justice. It was as though one had parachuted into the middle of a drama of the old South. With a little imagination, one could easily conjure a sweaty Tom Robinson and Atticus Finch vainly pleading their case before a hard-eyed jury of local white men—the ominous barred cell in the corner, mockingbirds flying in and out of the open windows.

The presiding judge was T. Werth Thagard, a soft-spoken, slight, white-haired man. His first act was to deny a defense motion to dismiss the indictment because of prejudicial pretrial publicity attributed to President Johnson's announcement of the defendant's arrest. He then quickly set about the business of choosing a jury.

After the first break, the judge announced that he had released the only black person on the panel, who had "privately" asked to be excused "because he had recently had some surgery done." While he did permit the prosecution to ask veniremen about their association with "secret organizations," he declined to excuse those who admitted they belonged to the klan or the white citizens' council. [7] "Gentlemen," he intoned, "the fact that you might

---

6   See photos 11 and 12.

7   White citizens councils were a network of white supremacist organizations formed in the

belong to any secret organization does not disqualify you, but is information which the lawyers are entitled to use in striking the jury."[8]

Over the prosecutor's objection, he also permitted defense counsel Murphy to inquire whether the jurors had heard President Johnson's announcement of the arrests and if they could possibly set aside the suggestion of guilt contained in the President's statement. But, in doing so, Murphy's words and actions went well beyond this facially legitimate inquiry. As though klan affiliation was a badge of honor, in virtually reverential tones he asked each group of prospective jurors if they had heard President Johnson say that the defendants were "members of the United Klans of America, Incorporated, Knights of the Ku Klux Klan?" Then, while Gamble sat and raised no objection, in a very long question and in fractured syntax, Murphy used grotesque body language, knowing looks, and pregnant intonations to suggest that the president had tried to convert this into a political trial and used his high office to lobby for a conviction:

> Let me ask you gentlemen this, if you heard this part of this thing: The President labeled the Klan a dirty band of bigots. He stated further that his father had fought Klansmen in Texas, and he had fought them all of his life and that he would continue to fight them?
>
> Let me ask you this question, gentlemen, and I address it to each man separately and severally. Of course, we know the President sits in the highest office in

---

mid-1950s to oppose integration and voting rights that primarily used economic retaliation against civil rights activists.

8   The Alabama "struck jury" selection system had been upheld on March 8, 1965, one day after Bloody Sunday. *Swain v. Alabama*, 380 U.S. 202 (1965). In other jurisdictions, the prosecutor and defense counsel are allowed to question prospective jurors about their views on subjects that could affect their objectivity, and to ask the judge to strike a potentially biased juror "for cause." These prosecutors and defense counsel then have a limited number of "preemptory challenges," which they can use to strike a juror for no reason. But in the Alabama system, jurors were rarely stricken "for cause" in 1965; instead, each counsel has a large number of "peremptory challenges." They take turns striking jurors using the information obtained from their questions, until only twelve jurors (plus a few alternates) remain. These latter strikes are solely at the lawyers' discretion. In *Swain*, the prosecutor struck the only six black candidates from the jury, which then found the black defendant guilty and sentenced him to death. Justice Byron White wrote the opinion upholding Alabama's system, over three dissenters including Chief Justice Earl Warren.

the United States of America, and the office is to be respected, and I would like to ask each one of you gentlemen. . . . Would the fact that the President of the United States of America, in making this statement, has said that these men are Klansmen, that they struck at night, that they were guilty, and that he charged them and convicted them and passed judgment without trial, by a man who holds high office, could that in any manner have any effect upon your delibera- tions, either consciously or unconsciously, that might tend in any manner, no matter how slight—to bias or prejudice you against this defendant?

As we watched Judge Thagard swear in the jurors who were finally produced by this biased selection process, there was no way to tell very much about them. Although blacks out-numbered whites by about 4 to 1 in Lowndes County, potential jurors were drawn from the very small pool of white men registered to vote there. To the naked eye they were virtually indistinguishable. The prosecutor had struck those who publicly admitted that they were members of either the klan or a white citizens' council and Murphy had struck some, but not all, of those who said they heard President Johnson's arrest announcement. One could only hope that his experience in Lowndes County gave prosecutor Gamble some slim chance of keeping out those who were trying to conceal themselves, get on the jury, and then act on their prejudice. On the other hand, the "klonsel," clearly a professional racist, was playing his role to the hilt.

The bottom line? This all white male jury had heard Murphy's repeated assertion that the defendant was a member of the klan. Some of them must have recognized imperial wizard Robert Shelton with his gaggle of grand dragons not just attending the trial but busily conferring with the defendant and handing notes to his counsel, and, of course, they had all heard Mur- phy's signal that this whole trial was a political witch hunt engineered by the klan's enemies in Washington, DC. All of this was Murphy's way of invok- ing the old Code of the South where juries were expected to protect those who preserved racial segregation, especially klansmen.

Chapter 6

BUILDING A MURDER CASE

Even as the selection of the jury proceeded Monday, pro-Klan, anti-Negro hand-bills were being circulated outside the courthouse.

Copies of one handbill . . . also were mailed late last week to many Lowndes County residents. County Solicitor Carlton Perdue said he and other county officials received copies.

The handbills, warning that forced integration would lead to bloodshed, declared that during Reconstruction Negroes could get by with "heinous" crimes because of unjust laws and "a black jury and judge."

The pamphlet declared that through "a secret organization the white men threw these unjust laws and orders to the winds, and in the dead of night, completely wiped out this tyranny."

—JACK NELSON, "ALL-WHITE JURY TO HEAR LIUZZO MURDER CASE," *LOS ANGELES TIMES*, MAY, 4, 1965, 1, 20

Long before the first witness takes the stand in a sensitive criminal prosecution, the contending lawyers calculate their plans as though they are military generals strategically plotting their soldiers' feints and charges. Prosecutor Gamble's plan of attack came after he carefully evaluated his battleground. While he recognized that local jurors would likely disfavor his side, he carefully tailored his presentation to try to get them to convict these Birmingham klansmen for exposing their Lowndes County to public ridicule. He had prosecuted cases in this county for years, and by experience had come to know this judge and jurors. He said he could predict almost exactly what would and would not "play" in Lowndes County.

As Gamble explained it to me, he designed his plan around several themes. First and foremost, he must convince the jurors that these renegade klansmen had no legitimate business at all in Lowndes County. They had driven the eighty miles from Birmingham just looking to stir up some trouble. By randomly seeing this white woman in Selma and then following and shooting her in Lowndes County, they had brought down shame, chaos, and dishonor on the people of Lowndes County. They were trespassers who flatly deserved to be punished.

Gamble also thought that he must not allow Murphy to sell the jurors on the notion that this trial was part of some political attack on Alabama's way of life that had been planned by the civil rights movement and directed from Washington, DC. Of course, there would have to be number of federal witnesses—Rowe, the major eyewitness, was a paid FBI informant and other FBI agents would have to testify about its detailed investigation of the crime. But his approach about protecting Lowndes County's reputation could still be presented and explained. And he would have to put on the other eyewitness, Leroy Moton, a black employee of Dr. King's SCLC, which had organized the march to Montgomery that went right through Lowndes County. Still, he laid plans to minimize the federal civil rights impact as much as possible.

To highlight that this was a crime against the State of Alabama that had been discovered and investigated by Alabama officials, the first five witnesses would be local men in blue—the two state troopers who were first on the scene, the Lowndes County Sheriff who would place the killing as taking place in Lowndes County, a state police investigator who had accompanied the victim's car to the state police facility for study, and the familiar face of the state police lieutenant who was a frequent witness in criminal cases in Lowndes County. The latter would testify about searching the victim's car and attending her autopsy.

While there was little, if any, chance of excluding any mention of the civil rights march, it certainly would not be a central part of the routine prosecution of a regular murder case. In examining Rowe, Gamble planned to limit his testimony just to his employment by the FBI, the actual shooting, and the immediately preceding events. Similarly, the examination of Leroy Moton would be strictly limited to the shooting out on the highway. By so narrowing this eyewitness testimony, Gamble could then ask the judge to enforce the usual rule and strictly limit Matt Murphy's cross-examination to the scope of the direct examination.[1]

In Moton's testimony there was also another way to safeguard the local prosecutor from seeming to sympathize with Mrs. Liuzzo's black passenger. Alabama Attorney General Richmond Flowers was one of very few state officials who publicly campaigned as a political moderate, and he had insisted that one of his deputies, Joe Breck Gantt, be assigned to assist Gamble in this prosecution. Moton's testimony was projected to be short and Gamble assigned Gantt to examine him. He planned to call Moton immediately after the first five state police witnesses.

Gamble did not plan to introduce any proof through testimony of family or friends to explain why the victim had traveled to Alabama. Evidence of the victim's conscience-driven trip to Selma would not be helpful to jurors in rural Lowndes County where virtually every white person knew about and disapproved of the civil rights march, and would neither understand nor agree with Viola Liuzzo's determination to go to Selma to offer help. He said that this would only stir up antagonism among the jurors.

Local newspapers, radio, TV, and even white churches had incessantly drummed that the marchers were left-wing radicals, including bearded communists and Jews, who were just using race issues to subvert basic American values. They would likely agree with Governor Wallace and southern editorialists that people who came to preach morality to Alabamians were hypocrites, who, if they really cared about racial issues, would stay at home and tend to the serious race problems in Detroit and other big northern cities. There, the story went, hundreds of thousands of blacks had been herded into dismal slums identified by high unemployment, a flourishing drug culture, and terrible "neighborhood" schools that were just as segregated as—and much more dangerous than—those in Alabama.

---

1   The cross-examination of a witness is normally limited to the scope of the original direct examination of the witness. On objection, the judge should restrain or set limits on the cross-examiner.

From Gamble's standpoint, there were very serious problems with Tommy Rowe as a trial witness. He was a professional snitch, paid by the FBI to come up with incriminating evidence against the klan. Rowe would be sorely tested to explain that he could be believed, when he had said and done things to maintain his status as a klansman while working to promote justice. The best approach would be to buttress his story with independent evidence confirming the truthfulness of his account. Gamble's plan was to sandwich Rowe between two state witnesses. The state medical examiner would testify that the victim had been shot in the head and that he had recovered the death bullet. Then Rowe would offer his vivid description of how defendant Wilkins had fired the first shots directly into the victim's car. The next witness, a state trooper, would then verify another part of Rowe's account, the state police stop of the murder car for the noisy muffler.

The remainder of the plan flowed from that point. Three FBI agents would testify that they found a group of "hulls" (what shell casings were called in rural Alabama) lying along the road right where Rowe said they would be. They would also testify to recovering a pistol from a warrant authorizing search of the Thomas house. Then, Rowe's FBI handler, Special Agent Neil Shanahan, would verify that Rowe was a reliable witness who regularly risked his life to help the Bureau, and who, before leaving, had contacted him for permission to go to Selma. Finally, an impressive FBI scientist, a ballistics expert, would positively match the Liuzzo death bullet as having been fired from the Thomas gun.

But, just before the first witness could be called to start this plan, defense counsel Murphy made a surprise motion. Under a rarely used Alabama trial court precedent, he demanded the right to interview the prosecution's two eyewitnesses, Rowe and Moton. Even though Murphy had been given all the FBI reports obtained from interviewing these witnesses, Judge Thagard ruled that under Alabama law the prosecution must produce its eyewitnesses for defense interviews before trial could begin, and he put the trial on hold until that was done.

I quickly called and arranged for Rowe to be brought from Maxwell Air Force Base in Montgomery. He was escorted into an office with Murphy, but flatly refused to talk to him. While he was present, Murphy served him with a state summons for a lawsuit to collect legal fees allegedly due for posting bail for Rowe to be released after his fake arrest by the FBI.[2]

Leroy Moton still had no legal counsel and was plainly upset at the prospect of having a two person tête-à-tête with the klan lawyer. He finally said he would do it, but only if I went with him, as I had when he first met with Gamble. Since this was much more visibility than was contemplated by my "liaison" role, I called Washington and was authorized to sit in on the interview. My understanding was that while I could not be Moton's legal adviser, my presence would encourage Moton to answer Murphy's questions and give Murphy notice that a federal representative would be able to testify about what transpired behind closed doors.

With the full courthouse watching and waiting, I escorted Moton down the hallway, past the Colored and White restrooms[3] and into the local office of Gamble's assistant prosecutor, County Solicitor Carlton Perdue, where he was to meet with Matt Murphy.

There was not much substance to this 15 minute "interview." I concluded that Murphy was more interested in intimidation than information and, in that, he partially succeeded. Moton became visibly upset and quarreled with Murphy over several totally insignificant matters—the speed of the Oldsmobile at specific times and certain phrases used by Moton. I listened carefully as they argued pointlessly. When it was finally over, I escorted Moton back through the sizeable white crowd that had gathered in the narrow hallways leading to the witness room.

---

2   I was told that FBI supervisory agents on their own had come up with this plan to have Rowe arrested with the other three klansmen. To the best of my knowledge, it was never discussed with Justice Department attorneys. I believe they were hoping that Murphy or one of the defendants would say something incriminating about the case, which Rowe could later testify about. But no admissions were made and later Murphy was able to cast aspersions at the Bureau for being dishonest and tricky.

3   Obviously, requiring a black witness to a crime to have to be escorted through a courthouse almost full of hostile whites, past segregated restrooms into an office that the white county solicitor is "loaning" to the klan klonsel could intimidate even the most determined witness. I was glad to be with Moton and sympathized with his reaction to Murphy's questions.

As we worked our way through the halls I had to ask people in the crowded halls to move aside so that we could pass through. Once, when we were stalled by the congestion, I called out "Excuse me, will you please let Mister Moton through." I had (knowingly, I confess) violated the local custom of always referring to a black person by using only a first name and absolutely no courtesy titles. One particularly obnoxious young local known to everyone as "Shorty" let out a rebel yell: "**Mister** Moton! **Mister** Moton!," he wailed loudly to the crowd, "Did y'all hear that? That Washington feller called that nigger boy **Mister** Moton." I scowled at the tormenter and we pushed on through.

As I was returning from the witness room, one of the kids who usually hung out with "Shorty" urgently hissed and beckoned me into a private conversation. He seemed a little sheepish and embarrassed for his buddy. Somehow he had learned my name: "Mr. Turner," he confided, "you shouldn't pay no 'tention to Shorty. He don't mean no harm. She-it," he drawled as though it explained everything, "Ol' Shorty's been fuckin' niggers since he was thirteen." Fifty years later, I am still baffled by this bizarre encounter.

PHOTOGRAPHS

The first five photographs are from the collection of James "Spider" Martin. In 1965 Martin covered events from Selma's Bloody Sunday through Dr. King's speech in Montgomery. This five-foot-two photographer, who frequently climbed to viewing spots, became a friend of Dr. King and followed him for several weeks. About fifty years later, his collection was acquired by the University of Texas. It has been featured at the Johnson Presidential Library and at shows in Selma and New York City. Originally, Spider complained that his conservative employer, Alabama's *Birmingham News*, would only publish his pictures on the paper's interior pages. His work shows the reality of the Civil Rights Movement more than any words can.

1. Hosea Williams and John Lewis confront troopers on Bloody Sunday. Photo © 1965 Spider Martin.

"There had been a two-minute warning, but like the old song went, 'there ain't no turning me 'round.' The troopers stampeded into the crowd beating everything in sight that was black. The marchers stood their ground, but were beaten down like dominos." —Spider Martin

2. Troopers Attack Peaceful Demonstrators on Bloody Sunday. Photo © 1965 Spider Martin.

"All of a sudden the troopers charged like a pack of wild dogs. Beating anyone in sight. Men, women, children, and me, Spider Martin. I can still feel the place on my head. He fractured John Lewis' skull [in light coat with backpack]. The tear gas was everywhere. Screaming. Billy clubs waving in the air. The troopers were mad dogs. This moment changed the dynamics of Alabama, the USA, and the world forever. This was Bloody Sunday." —Spider Martin

3. Trooper standing over March leader. Photo © 1965 Spider Martin.

"Amelia Boynton Robinson was beaten unconscious. I have always wondered what the state trooper was thinking." —Spider Martin

4. On the March (L to R): John Lewis, Dr. Martin Luther King Jr., Ralph Abernathy, and James Bevel. Photo © 1965 Spider Martin.

"When I first saw this old antebellum mansion near Haynesville on Highway 80 I thought this house represented 400 years of slavery. The house even still had the slave quarters out back." —Spider Martin

5. Dr. Martin Luther King Jr., Speaking to Triumphant Marchers, Alabama Capitol, Montgomery, March 25, 1965. Photo © 1965 Spider Martin.

"This was the end of an era and the beginning of another." —Spider Martin

6. King Memorial, Selma, Alabama. Photo © 2015 James C. Turner.

The Brown Chapel AME Church served as headquarters for the Selma to Montgomery Freedom March. James Reeb, Viola Liuzzo, and Jimmy Lee Jackson are also remembered.

7. Victim Viola Liuzzo and family. Photo by Getty Images.

The Detroit mother of five came to Selma because "[t]his is something I must do."

8. Death vehicle, U.S. Route 80, Lowndes County, Alabama. Photo © Bruce Davidson/Magnum Photos.

After klansmen's fatal gunfire completely shattered the driver-side window, the Liuzzo car drifted from the highway and stopped.

9. Viola Liuzzo Memorial, U.S. Route 80, Lowndes County, Alabama. Photo © 2015 James C. Turner.

Erected by the SCLC at the site where klansmen shot and killed Mrs. Liuzzo on March 25, 1965, after the Selma to Montgomery Freedom March.

10. Hayneville Courthouse. Photo © 2015 James C. Turner.

This antebellum (1856) Lowndes County structure was the site of the first two Liuzzo trials and the Jonathan Daniels murder proceedings in 1965. Note Confederate memorial in foreground.

11. Lowndes County courtroom. Photo © 2015 James C. Turner.

Author revisiting the courtroom fifty years after state murder trials of klansmen resulted in an acquittal.

12. Courtroom prisoner cage. Photo © 2015 James C. Turner.

A chilling relic of times when defendants were publicly displayed in open holding cells; now unused, this cage remains on display in the Lowndes County courtroom to this day.

COURTROOM PICTURES OF THE KLAN MURDER TRIAL
Defense Lawyer Matt Murphy's victory sign

MAY 21 · 1965 · 35¢

13. Klan Klonsel Matt Murphy. Photo by Robert W. Kelley/The LIFE Picture Collection/Getty Images.

Featured on the cover of LIFE Magazine sending V for Victory with the only fingers on his right hand, while Murphy's left hand displays his "NEVER" button, outside Haynesville courthouse after parading around the town square with the accused klansmen, wizards, and dragons.

14. Eyewitness Leroy Moton outside the courthouse. Photo © 1965 Spider Martin.

This SCLC worker was a passenger in the car driven by Mrs. Liuzzo.

15. FBI informant Gary Thomas Rowe (left) and FBI Special Agent Neil Shanahan, May 3, 1965. Photo by Getty Images/Bettman.

Rowe was an eyewitness riding in the car with the klansmen who shot and killed Mrs. Liuzzo. Shanahan was his FBI handler.

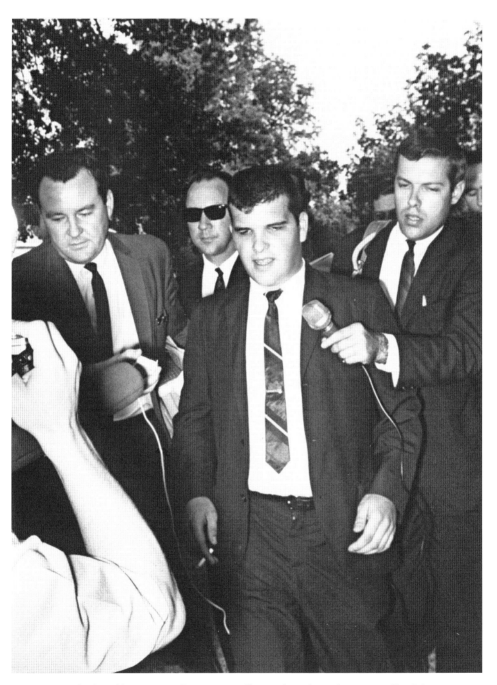

16. Defendant klansman Collie Leroy Wilkins. Photo by Robert W. Kelley/The LIFE Picture Collection/Getty Images.

FBI informant Rowe identified Wilkins as firing shots "point-blank" into the car driven by Mrs. Liuzzo, and ballistic analysis matched shell casings found on the scene with the klansman's handgun.

17. U.S. District Judge Frank M. Johnson Jr. Photo by Getty Images/Bettmann.

One of the most respected jurists in the country, Judge Johnson presided over the federal conspiracy trial of the klansmen who shot Mrs. Liuzzo, and sentenced each to the maximum ten-year prison term allowed.

18. John Doar (l) and the author. Photo from author's collection.

In awarding Doar the Medal of Freedom on May 29, 2012, President Obama described his stellar record across the South from 1963 to 1967, concluding, "And I think it is fair to say that I would not be here if it had not been for his work."

19. Doar's secret weapon. Justice Department photo from author's collection.

D. Robert Owen, a tireless lawyer, who rose to Deputy Assistant Attorney General, ran the Division's boiler room in the Liuzzo case and in 1967 became the lead counsel in the Mississippi Burning case. He died on January 2, 1981.

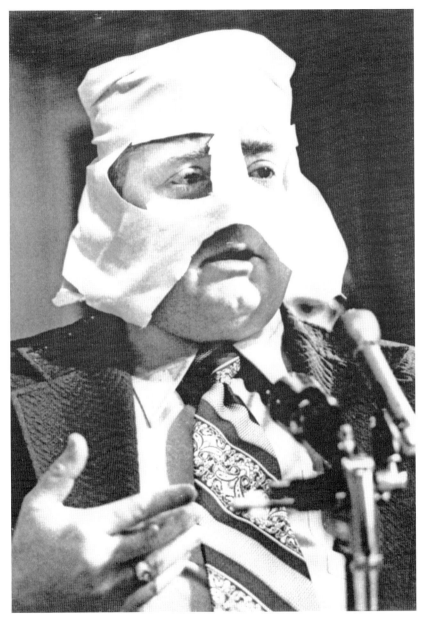

20. Tommy Rowe appearing before the U.S. Senate Intelligence Committee. Photo by Bride Lane Library/Popperfoto/Getty Images.

The former informant was allowed to appear in a mask to give testimony before the Church Committee on February 12, 1976. The Committee Report was the basis for the new Levi Guidelines on managing informants.

21. With the Reverend Jesse Jackson (r) at 25th anniversary of Bloody Sunday. Photo from author's collection.

As Acting Assistant Attorney General, the author delivered the speech printed in the appendix in Montgomery, Alabama, on March 7, 1990.

22. President Obama and John Lewis lead Selma marchers. Official White House photo by Lawrence Jackson.

Commemorating the 50th anniversary of the Selma to Montgomery March, March 7, 2015.

Chapter 7

TRIAL DAY TWO
The Eyewitnesses Rack Up Points

> *[A]fter the killing . . . Eugene Thomas suggested, "Let's go by the Dragon's house and tell him what a good job we did."*
>
> *"What did you do to Mrs. Liuzzo while you were there in the car?" Matt H. Murphy Jr., the defense counsel who is a klansman asked. "Nothing," Mr. Moton replied.*
>
> *"Did you reach over there and touch her," Mr. Murphy asked. "No."*
>
> *"Did you lay your hand on her?" "No."*
>
> —ROY REED, "F.B.I. INFORMER TELLS COURT KLANSMEN SHOT MRS. LIUZZO," *NEW YORK TIMES*, MAY 5, 1965, I, 33

On Tuesday, May 4, 1965, Judge Thagard formally opened the trial with the traditional pronouncement: "Mr. Solicitor, you may put the case to the jury." Prosecutor Gamble read the brief, but curiously worded, indictment for first-degree murder as issued by the Lowndes County Grand Jury, which charged "that before the finding of this indictment, Collie Leroy Wilkins, whose name to the grand jury is otherwise unknown, unlawfully, and with malice aforethought, killed Viola Gregg Liuzzo by shooting her with a pistol, against the peace and dignity of the State of Alabama."

After a terse, fact-based opening statement, lead prosecutor Gamble called the first Alabama state trooper and began to follow his witness plan. But defense counsel Matt Murphy interfered, promptly unveiling the basic elements of his strategy. He would try to confuse every state witness, relate every possible testimonial fact to the "communist civil rights march," and, whenever possible, feed local prejudices by relentlessly attacking the character of the murder victim.

The direct testimony of the initial Alabama lawmen went as planned, but Murphy took a wild swipe at each one. Referring to a fuzzy blowup of the jumbled interior of the victim's car after it was brought in from where it had crashed after the shooting, he asked one trooper about a mysterious "tube that appears so openly in this photograph." In fact, the tube was pretty plainly a common burn medicine called "Unguentine." While its label may have been a little hard to read in the slightly dim photo, Murphy tried his best to plant the seed that this might be a "dangerous" drug. When the officer said he had paid no attention to the container, Murphy portrayed incredulity by raising his voice and his eyebrows and pantomimed a knowing look to the jury.[1]

The klan klonsel then pointed to another item in the blurry picture, actually the victim's coat with two visible buttons, suggesting that it resembled a "transmitter" or some other "instrument." Repeatedly, he tried to lead the officer to "see" that the buttons were really control knobs, a loose button thread really a connecting wire. But each witness rejected his suggestion. The sinister "device," they said, was nothing more than just a coat and some buttons. Undaunted, and with absolutely no foundation, Murphy launched another missile: "Did you find a .38 pistol in the glove compartment?" When the officer said he hadn't, Murphy quickly asked, "Did you look in the glove compartment?" When the witness said he did not (the car was searched by other officers), Murphy again turned to the jury and rolled his eyes knowingly.

At first I was outraged that the prosecutor would let all this go unchallenged. My only thought was that maybe Gamble was playing out the rope he hoped Murphy would use to hang his client. While it was a stretch, he could have been counting on the jurors to realize that the klan lawyer's out-

---

1   Although it was not referred to by either side, there were three other innocuous "tubes" contained in the official inventory of the victim's car: "1 tube of first aid cream" and "2 tubes of epoxy-Elmer glue."

rageous questions and maneuvers were desperation ploys that revealed the absence of any real defense.

But, Murphy continued his baiting, either oblivious or indifferent to the possibility that jurors might catch on. He tried to suggest that the FBI had taken over the forensic examination of the victim's vehicle, thus giving Bureau Agents a clear opportunity to "plant" evidence. In response the state police insisted that the entire search of the car not only had been done jointly by the two agencies but was also conducted in a State of Alabama facility.

Finally, he threw another "hail Mary" when an Alabama police lieutenant said the victim's purse contained a "driver's license, various cards." Glancing knowingly at the jury box, the klonsel pounced: "Cards. Did you see a Communist membership card in that purse?" The judge overruled the prosecutor's lack of foundation objection as the jurors quickly leaned forward only to hear the state lieutenant firmly answer, "No, sir."

The stage was now set for Leroy Moton, the passenger in the car and the prosecution's first eyewitness to the murder. I had spent a good bit of time with Moton and had come to like him a lot. Nineteen years old, his build was similar to my own at that age—my mother always called me a "bean pole." He was six foot four but weighed only about 130 pounds. He wore thick, horn-rimmed glasses that magnified his eyes. He had dropped out of Selma's segregated high school and still lived with his mother in the "project." Moton was a very serious, soft-spoken young man who neither smoked nor drank. Although his communication skills were somewhat limited, he was bright and totally honest.

Like many southern blacks living in segregated Alabama, Moton had no experience with the court system and was extremely nervous to be the only black witness in a white-run trial in a dangerous, hostile county. While I had done what I could to calm him, Alabama Assistant Attorney General Gantt, who would question him on the stand, had only allocated time for one friendly but perfunctory interview with him, not nearly enough time to earn Moton's confidence. Once on the witness stand, after establishing that he had been riding in the death car, Gantt simply asked Moton to relate "anything unusual" that had happened on the highway that night. The teenager's response quickly became garbled and was barely audible. Murphy whined loudly, "Judge, I can't hear a thing he is saying," and the judge directed Moton to "talk a little louder."

Moton then became visibly unnerved by the objection and the judge's prodding and overreacted by beginning to articulate each word at an unnaturally loud volume and slowed his delivery, as though he was speaking to a foreigner. He finished a very truncated, confusing account of the shooting: "and approaching further on toward Montgomery a car pulled up side of us and shot in the car two or three times, and the car was going off the road and I stopped the car." After the damage was done, Gantt abandoned asking for narration and finished the direct examination by going through what happened bit by bit.

The idea that Murphy's cross-examination would be confined, as required by Alabama law, to the narrow scope of Moton's direct testimony quickly flew out of the open windows of the courtroom. When Moton said he worked for the SCLC, Murphy immediately asked who headed that organization (Dr. Martin Luther King Jr.). Murphy asked whether Mrs. Liuzzo had been in the demonstration on March 25 at the state capitol building; the answer was yes. Whenever he pronounced the victim's name Murphy would screw up his face and slowly form each syllable—playing on anti-Catholic and anti-Italian bias, "Lye-oooze-zoh"—as though it was a word from another language and was difficult or distasteful to say.

Moton said he first saw Viola Liuzzo that day at St. Jude's Hospital in Montgomery. This was a wonderful Catholic institution named for the patron saint of difficult or hopeless causes. It was known to everyone around as one of Montgomery's few integrated facilities and was certainly the only one that offered the same medical treatment to blacks and whites. It was also widely known that St. Jude's was on the fringe of town and had befriended the marchers. In fact, it hosted a star-studded Hollywood gala the last night of the march and served as the assembly point for the final leg of the march into Montgomery. Hospital insiders told me later that because of these actions helping the marchers, within the next few months St. Jude's Hospital would lose most of its white physicians, its white patronage, and much of its financial support and start a long, slow decline.

But Murphy could not care less about St. Jude's work. Instead, he asked Moton to confirm that this was a "Catholic hospital," and therefore a traditional klan target. Then he casually queried, "Is that a nigger hospital or is that a white hospital?" The prosecutor's objection to that question was sustained, but with absolutely no comment from Judge Thagard.

When Moton explained how they had then carried a carload of Marchers back to Selma, Murphy wanted to know the race, gender, and seating location of each and every person in the car. His point was to show that in the car blacks and whites, males and females, had all been jammed together, all obscenely rubbing against one another.

A minor tug of war over diction developed during this exchange. Murphy only referred to members of the black race with two words: "Nigras" and "niggers." He never said the word Negroes, but sometimes would use the segregationist enunciation "Nig-ras." The official transcript shows that the court reporter would render this "Nigras" as "Negroes," thereby distinguishing it from Murphy's other, and much more customary term, the uncapitalized word "niggers." Of course, Moton was offended deeply by Murphy's words, and in answering about the race of the car's passengers, he took great care to highlight Murphy's denigrating "Nig-ras" by using and pointedly stressing the correct pronunciation—"knee-grows."

To me this was a shocking example of our country's sectional language problems. In this context an objection would never be raised or even thought about. The white jurors understood Murphy perfectly and, clearly, the judge had no interest in curbing racial insults in his courtroom.

Murphy then led the witness on a contentious rehash of the drive from Selma to the place of the shooting. They haggled over everything—the speed of the cars, the distance between them, exactly where the Olds was when the shots came. Things reached a breaking point when he asked Moton about leaning over to tune the radio. Still shaken by his near-death experience, Moton's answers became curt, almost testy. He explained about tuning the radio to get a particular Nashville station and Murphy asked him what "Mrs. Lye-ooze-zoh" was doing at that time.

I had heard Moton's account many times and it was always a simple, no-frills rendering of the facts. So, I virtually did a double take when I heard

him almost mumble: "She was humming 'We Shall Overcome.'" Murphy
heard it, too, but he wanted to make absolutely sure it registered clearly with
the jury. He turned quickly to the bench, whining "Judge, I couldn't hear
what the man said." The judge nodded and, in a patronizing tone—using
only Moton's first name—"Would you mind repeating that, Leroy?" Moton
restated it slightly louder, and the klonsel was off and running, openly mocking the witness:

Q   She just started singing that, "We Shall Overcome"? What's the rest of
    the words that she was singing?
A   She was just singing "We Shall Overcome"
Q   [In a mocking tone] We shall overcome, we shall overcome, we shall
    overcome, just over and over again?
A   We shall overcome someday and then come back to the point.
Q   What point?
A   We shall overcome.
Q   What are you trying to overcome?

Much too late to serve any realistic purpose, the judge finally sustained
Prosecutor Gamble's objection to further dissection of the civil rights hymn.

Murphy then moved on to a new quibble, this one about the speed of the
Liuzzo car. Moton said he did not know its speed when the car left the road
and Murphy tried to "refresh his recollection" by calling attention to his and
Moton's court-ordered pretrial interview earlier that day. Moton answered
by stating (correctly) that in their interview it was Murphy himself that had
suggested the car's speed: "You set the point," he said, and further reminded
Murphy that "Mr. Turner was in there with us, too."

Accepting Moton's formulation, Murphy then asked whether "in response to my question didn't you say that you were going 65 or 70?" You
could hear the quick intake of breath among the courtroom spectators when
they heard Moton's sharply delivered and totally unexpected answer: "That's
right, but you were being so rude I had to agree with you some way."

Murphy was absolutely indignant and righteously thundered: "Judge, I
move to strike that remark." Instantly, and with a very disapproving tone,

the judge agreed: "Yes, that motion is granted." In Matt Murphy's book of southern etiquette, he had just scored a very important point. He had goaded young Moton into being "uppity" by daring to call a white man "rude" even though in fact he had been just that. The judge instantly rebuked the witness.

The relentless klonsel moved on. After the shooting, Moton said he did not know her condition, but saw that Mrs. Liuzzo was "kind of tilted over." In an almost friendly, conversational tone Murphy leaned forward to inquire: "Did you smell any whiskey on her breath?" But he was not friendly when he moved on to suggest Moton might have molested the dead white woman after the shooting:

Q   What did you do to Mrs. Liuzzo while you were there in the car?
A   I didn't do anything to Mrs. Liuzzo while I was in the car.
Q   Did you reach over there and touch her?
A   No I didn't.
Q   You didn't do what?
A   Touch her.
Q   You didn't touch her? You didn't lay your hands on her?
A   No, sir.
Q   And you were there in the car with her for 30 minutes?
A   That's right.

Murphy then suggested that Moton had fired the shots into the windshield, snatched a wad of money from the victim's purse, and then had run down the road. Moton was so scandalized at Murphy's charges that his spontaneous denial rang absolutely true: "I did not fire no shots through the windshield and I did not go through her pocketbook and get no money, and I didn't have a gun and I didn't do anything. You are trying to pin something on me; that's what you are trying to do." Any truth-seeker would have been instantly convinced by Moton's righteous reaction to this slanderous series of questions. But most of the local observers in that old southern courtroom brought with them such biased opinions on racial issues that they could never accept that here was an honest witness who, on this point at least, was speaking the absolute truth.

When I first heard about the ku klux klan as a boy in Colorado, I was told that its three Ks phonetically identified the three minorities it targeted— koons, kikes, and katholics.[2] In his final sortie against Moton, the klonsel uncovered a way to insult Jews, the only scapegoat group he had not yet ridiculed. Moton testified that he had run for several miles before being picked up by a truck loaded with returning marchers and that the truck was driven by a Rabbi. Murphy instantly zoomed in on the Rabbi, his brow furrowed, his eyes squinted each time he spoke that title:

Q   Now who did you come in contact with?
A   With a Rabbi from Boston.
Q   With a Rabbi?
A   That's right.
Q   Who was that Rabbi with?
A   About twenty other people.
Q   Were they white people or black people?
A   It was an integrated truck.
Q   An integrated truck [incredulously]?
A   Yes, sir.
Q   Then there were whites and Negroes both in that truck?
A   That's right.
Q   And a Rabbi driving the truck?
A   That's right.
Q   You mean a Rabbi who teaches a Jewish congregation, is that what you mean?
A   Yes.
Q   A synagog [sic]. You know what a synagog is, don't you?
A   I think so.

---

2   As a native of Colorado, I have been surprised to read how the klan had been active in that state until it faded out around 1927. There were no lynchings, but a lot of noise. The klan was centered in Canon City, about 30 miles from Pueblo where I grew up. During the 1920s the state's governor, one of its senators, and other local officials were alleged to be members. See Ed Quillen, "Kolorado Klan Kountry," *Colorado Springs Independent*, May 22, 2003, and Robert Alan Goldberg, *Hooded Empire: The Ku Klux Klan in Colorado* (Urbana: University of Illinois Press, 1981).

Q A Rabbi teaches in a synagog. You have been to a synagog, haven't you?

A No.

Q Was this Rabbi dressed up in a Rabbi's uniform?

A No, he wasn't.

Q What kind of uniform did he have on?

A He just had on plain clothes.

Q Who was that Rabbi?

The judge finally sustained Gamble's long overdue objection and shut off further probing questions about the Rabbi from Boston, commenting, "I think you have covered it pretty well."

I joined **Mister** Moton after he left the stand and gave him my sincere thanks for his testimony. With only minimal help from either the prosecutor or the judge, he had been able to hold his own under some very trying conditions. For the most part he was respectful and I thought his legitimate outrage at some of Murphy's gross suggestions was very persuasive. After I thanked him for his help, he headed on back to Selma—along with a bearded white guy dressed in bib overalls and beach sandals.

The next witness was Dr. Paul Schoffeit, the state toxicologist, who performed the autopsy on Mrs. Liuzzo. He identified and testified to removing a bullet from the victim's head and transmitting it to the FBI for a ballistics analysis. Murphy had little success with this witness on scientific or technical matters. However, with knowing looks at the jury, he did get the doctor to confirm that the body and clothing were not very fresh and that the victim was wearing a girdle but no panties. Her blood contained a sedative, phenobarbital, and a vaginal smear was negative for sexual activity. In a parting shot, Murphy had the doctor confirm that this negative smear would not be conclusive if "some contraceptive device" had been used. At this he favored the jury with another of his self-satisfied leers and resumed his seat.

The day's last witness was the FBI informant, Tommy Rowe. Everyone present—jurors, spectators, and media—leaned forward to get a glimpse of this undercover man who claimed he had watched the klan commit a murder. Rowe was neatly dressed in coat and tie and I remember being pleased at his businesslike appearance. But for the jacket straining a bit over his paunch, he actually gave a pretty fair imitation of an FBI agent. He had spent the last few days working with Special Agent Shanahan on witness demeanor, and it showed. When he took the oath, he raised his right hand, turned his blue eyes directly on the jurors and resolutely answered "I do," perhaps just a shade too loudly.

Rowe's direct testimony approached textbook clarity and demeanor. He thought before speaking and, very like an agent, called the prosecutor "sir" at least once in almost every response. The testimony began with the klan group's arrival in Montgomery and proceeded through the day's various activities. When the klan car finally caught up with the Liuzzo Oldsmobile after U.S. 80 had narrowed to a two-lane road, the prosecutor asked "just tell us what happened when you started around the car." The entire room was quiet, listening intently to his response:

> We started around this automobile and Wilkins told him, says you get up side of the automobile, it won't take but a minute to stop it. Gene said all right, you all get ready, and I said what are you going to do? Force him off the road? He said wait and see. He pulled around right beside of the automobile.
>
> As we got directly even with the automobile Wilkins said give it some gas, and Gene sped up just a little ahead of the other automobile, put the rear window of our automobile immediately beside the window of the driver of the other automobile. Wilkins had his arm out the window, with the windows down on that side, the front and back—Wilkins put his arm out the window to approximately elbow distance.
>
> And just as we got even with the front window there was a lady driving the automobile; she looked around at the automobile, directly facing the automobile we were in, she looked directly at us. Just as she looked at us Wilkins fired two shots through the window in the front of her automobile.

Rowe further testified that after the first two shots Thomas yelled, "all right, men, shoot the hell out of them." Eaton and Wilkins then emptied their weapons and Rowe testified that he had stuck his arm out the window and pretended to fire.

Rowe's account was spontaneous and very credible. His body language, frequent gestures, and even his searching and stumbling over a few words projected the clear image of someone concentrating very hard to come up with every last detail.

When Rowe's direct testimony ended, Judge Thagard announced that cross-examination would not take place until the following morning. "Mr. Murphy," he explained, "has already told me during the recess that he would prefer when he begins his cross-examination that it not be broken into.... I think we should accede to his request."

All in all the first day was fairly good for the prosecution. The official state witnesses had established that this was in fact an Alabama crime, and the prosecution's two eyewitnesses had told compelling stories of a political assassination in America.

Chapter 8

TRIAL DAY THREE
Murphy Takes on the Feds

The third day of the trial drew the largest crowd of spectators thus far. The court-room, an unscreened second-floor chamber that admits birds as well as breezes, was almost filled with residents of Lowndes County.

Many of the spectators showed their sympathy for the defendant by fraternizing during recesses with Robert M. Shelton Jr., the Tuscaloosa man who heads the United Klans of America and Robert Creel of Birmingham, the Alabama Grand Dragon of the organization.

—ROY REED, "KLANSMAN LINKED TO DEATH BULLET,"
NEW YORK TIMES, MAY 6, 1965, 24

Matt Murphy's cross-examination of Rowe began with a low-key review of Rowe's background. Murphy paused here and there to get in a dig. When Rowe said he had been born and raised in Savannah, Murphy tried to plant the idea that Rowe had been active in the civil rights movement in Georgia: "Did you know Hosea Williams [an aide to Dr. King] over there?" Rowe said he did not. Under Murphy's questioning, Rowe claimed not to know where his wife and children were living, but I suspect he did know but was not going to reveal that information to the klan for fear they would threaten his kids.

Murphy took him through his recruitment as a paid informant. Rowe claimed that he wasn't doing it just for the money, but because the FBI had asked him to help. Murphy demanded to know how much he had been paid each year and Rowe estimated that it totaled about $5,000 per year. Murphy's subsequent references to the "thousands" of dollars Rowe had been paid caused Gamble on redirect to introduce the 87 receipts, each one signed by Rowe, for a total of just over $13,000 for the entire five years of work.[1]

Murphy then moved on to one of his main defenses—that by testifying against the klan Rowe was violating the "sacred oath" he had sworn when he joined its membership, thereby suggesting he was not worthy of belief. "Did you hold up your right hand and swear before God certain matters?," Murphy asked. When the witness agreed that he had taken an oath, Murphy stood at attention, his solemn voice ringing throughout the courtroom, his mangled right hand raised high, as he recited from memory the klan oath, surely one of the fraternal world's most repetitious and childish:

> I most solemnly swear that I will forever keep sacredly secret the signs, words and grip, and any and all other matters and knowledge of the Order [united klans of America] regarding which a most rigid secrecy must be maintained . . . which may at any time be communicated to me and will never divulge same nor ever cause same to be divulged to any person in the whole world, unless I know positively that such person is a member of this Order in good and regular standing, and not even then unless it be for the best interests of this Order. I most sacredly vow and most positively swear that I will never yield to bribe, flattery, threats, passion, punishment, persecution, persuasion, nor any other enticements whatever coming from or offered by any person or persons, male or female, for the purpose of obtaining from me a secret or secret information. I will die rather than divulge the same, so help me God.

As Murphy droned on with this tedious oath, I was struggling to keep a straight face. The klan's "sacred oath" sounded to me as though it had been composed by a band of ten year olds playing in their cardboard club house while chanting "cross my heart and hope to die, stick a needle in my eye." Murphy, of course, never suggested how the FBI could obtain reliable klan

---

1 In retrospect, Gamble probably should have introduced the receipts when he first presented his evidence to the court, instead of allowing even an arguable appearance that Murphy had forced the prosecution into some "embarrassing" disclosure.

information without allowing its informants to make false oaths of allegiance. But as I glanced around the room at the white jurors and audience, I abruptly realized that almost everyone was listening in a very attentive and respectful manner. It was hard to believe, but Murphy's delivery of this ridiculous oath seemed to be connecting with Lowndes County residents and likely would be given serious consideration by the jury.

But it seemed impossible for Murphy to stop even when he was ahead. Almost immediately he was back flailing away and drawing objections from Gamble: "Now during this time you considered yourself . . . as an undercover man or a pimp, is that correct?" "Were you a member of the National Association for the Advancement of Colored People?" "Did you have any other connections down here in Selma with any individuals and made plans to kill this woman?" "Did you have any contact with Carl Braden [a reputed communist at the Highlander Folk School in Tennessee]?" Or with "Martin Luther King?" "Did you make a statement . . . in November, 1964, that you were a card carrying member of the Communist Party?" The very idea of blustery, hard-drinking Tommy Rowe as a practicing Marxist would boggle any serious mind. Many of the objections were sustained and Rowe calmly denied the remainder.

The real fireworks started when Rowe was asked about what happened in Murphy's office on the day after the shooting. In order to conceal Rowe's identity until the other three klansmen had been apprehended, the FBI arrest warrants had included Rowe's name as a defendant and, in fact, he had not been arrested but had been placed into what the Bureau reports called "simulated" custody. Later, a $50,000 bond was set for each of the defendants and Murphy posted bail for all of them, including Rowe.

When he was released, Rowe went straight to Murphy's law office and, following the instructions of his FBI handlers, told Murphy that the FBI had tried to tempt him with a large sum of money. On the stand Murphy asked, "if you didn't tell me this in the office: That the Federal Bureau of Investigation had offered to give you 900 acres in Minnesota, which was a farm, and give you sufficient money to run that farm on for the rest of your life if you would co-operate with them in helping to break the back of the United Klans of America?"

The judge overruled Gamble's objection and Rowe replied: "I would like to answer that. No, sir, Mr. Murphy, you instructed me to put that information out." Murphy's voice rose in consternation. He quickly shouted: "Are you saying that I told you that?" Rowed replied: "That's correct, Mr. Murphy." Murphy asked again and got the same answer. His face flushed deeply. He appeared to be totally out of control. As Judge Thagard repeatedly banged his gavel for attention, Murphy lost it completely and acted out a real scene. He grabbed his snapped-brim straw hat from the counsel table, first slapped it on the table, then raised it above his head and slammed it to the floor. He advanced toward Rowe, waving his arms, his three-fingered hand clenched into a fist. Prosecutor Gamble quickly asked for a recess and the judge responded indulgently, but with absolutely no criticism of Murphy's conduct: "I'll give you time to cool off, Mr. Murphy."

Rowe ultimately was allowed to explain that in order to conceal his undercover status, he had told Murphy a fictitious story that the FBI had offered him "500 acres of apples." Murphy really liked the idea of the FBI trying to bribe a witness and agreed, saying, "let's make it 550 acres and . . . $160,000." Murphy immediately and outrageously challenged Rowe's account, shouting: "Would you be willing to take a lie detector test with me on that particular point?" But the judge sustained Gamble's objection and Rowe was not allowed to answer.

Tommy Rowe had been under cross-examination for about an hour and forty-five minutes. He had defended his shocking tale of watching a cold-blooded murder and included many details susceptible of verification by the independent witnesses before and after. Murphy had thrown everything at him and had made a few points. For example, Rowe was not asked about why he had fired no shots when Thomas ordered the klansmen to shoot, or whether he threw out any unfired shells onto the road, or how he had described the place where they were thrown and later found by FBI agents. Finally, only the jurors could judge the impact of the false klan oath, his status as a paid informant, and Murphy's sensational quarrel with Rowe over the land in Minnesota.

Chapter 9

TRIAL DAY FOUR
A Twenty-Minute Defense, a Timeless Argument

*Murphy called no witnesses to refute [the state's evidence]. In his harangue he
implied that Mrs. Liuzzo was a whore, that Rowe was a traitor and that Moton
was a liar. The rambling, violent character of his summation made a tragicomedy
out of the trial, and even some of the Alabama jurors seemed to be dismayed by it.*

—"PICTORIAL SUMMATION OF A TRAGICOMIC MISTRIAL,"
LIFE MAGAZINE, MAY 21, 1965, 33

At the end of day three, prosecutor Gamble finished with the last of the
federal witnesses, the FBI firearms expert who positively identified as the
murder weapon the gun agents had obtained after executing a search warrant at the Eugene Thomas house. After thinking about it overnight, on
Thursday morning, May 6, Gamble announced to the judge that the state's
case was now complete. Murphy professed great shock at this and pleaded
for a fifteen-minute break "to get myself organized for the defense." Judge
Thagard invited him to "take whatever time you need." and the klonsel
responded that if he just had the fifteen minutes, "I'll really roll."

After the break, when everyone had resumed their places, one of the
most unusual courtroom events I have ever witnessed occurred. One of the
jurors was standing in the jury box, raising his hand. When recognized by
the judge, the juror respectfully requested an explanation of three points:
"the condition of Mr. Rowe when the agent talked to him in Birmingham"
after the shooting; "if there were any finger prints on the shell cases" the

agents had recovered near the highway; and, "if there were finger prints on the . . . murder weapon."[1]

Judge Thagard received the juror's inquiry without comment and asked prosecutor Gamble if he could present any evidence on the points raised. Gamble said he could and would bring in witnesses within ten minutes. Then FBI Special Agent Shanahan testified that Rowe had appeared totally sober, the agent who obtained the murder weapon testified that he had not requested that it be examined for prints because he knew it had been handled by several people, and, the firearms examiner said the casings—which had also been rained on and handled—had not been examined.

The juror had a point, and perhaps the questions about these tests made sense, but the agents said that, under the pressure of the search, they honestly did not think that further tests would produce anything.[2] In fact, an agent later advised me privately that the FBI had disciplined at least one of the agents who had been involved in this search.

There was still one other preliminary matter before Murphy presented his "really roll" defense. He asked for and received permission to recall Rowe, saying this new evidence required more "cross-examination." But, this, it turned out, was just another excuse for Murphy to deliver a long speech in front of the jury about the farm in Minnesota, arguing again just how seriously Rowe's statement had slandered him. During his "question," which went on for almost five minutes, Murphy again became agitated, spoke loudly, and vigorously waved his arms some more. He said he was entitled to clear this matter up and again offered to pay for a lie detector test for Rowe

---

1   Alabama appears to be one of only three states that allow jurors to ask questions during a criminal prosecution (see Peter DeFilippis, "Should Jurors Be Allowed to Ask Questions at Trial?," *New York Personal Injury* blog, March 8, 2013).

2   There were also other problems with the search of the Thomas house. The searching agents also found and seized klan robes from a closet and a whip and chain wrapped in clothes hidden behind the water heater. Unfortunately, these items could not be introduced into evidence because the federal warrant had stated they were looking for "firearms." Since the federal statute deals with conspiracy, not murder, hindsight suggests that the warrant should have been directed to find "firearms or klan paraphernalia." Any experienced agent drafting a search warrant for a conspiracy violation should know how to identify all relevant evidence.

and himself. When Gamble finally objected to what Murphy was doing, the judge agreed he should stop rehashing these same old questions, but only with the rather tepid reminder that "we are not trying you, Mr. Murphy." In many trial courts such an unprofessional outburst would at least have merited an instruction to the jury to disregard it, or perhaps warning of a reprimand or possible contempt citation if such misconduct continued.

Murphy was now ready to "really roll" into the case for the defense. In over sixty years at the bar, this was the flimsiest effort by a defense counsel I have ever sat through. The entire trial transcript (without closing arguments) totals 432 pages. The defense that Murphy had needed extra time to carefully "organize" accounts for only ten pages. His first witness was Robert Shelton, the imperial wizard of the united klans of America. Shelton, who had sat right behind the defendant throughout the trial, frequently passing notes to Murphy, had no real evidence to give. He was there to confirm publicly that this had been a klan operation and that Shelton agreed with Murphy that it was Rowe who first brought up the farm in Minnesota.

Next, Murphy called Robert Thomas, grand dragon of the Eastview klavern and another man who was a member of that klavern. Both testified to the same effect about the Minnesota farm but said nothing about the Liuzzo murder. Murphy then asked another klansman whether Rowe had attacked him with a pistol in March, but Gamble's objection was sustained, and the witness was dismissed after saying nothing.

The so-called alibi witness, Lorene Frederick, said she did know the four klansmen and that they had been in her club in Birmingham for beer the night of the murder "around 9:30 or 10:00 o'clock," but quickly added that this was her "impression," which she "couldn't swear to." On cross-examination, she admitted that it could have been sometime "after 10:00 o'clock." Murphy's last gasp was to ask another woman whether sometime in 1963 Rowe told her he was a "card carrying member of the Communist Party." The judge sustained Gamble's hearsay objection and she was not permitted to answer.

That was it! Murphy's vaunted defense was that there was no defense, legal or factual. His alibi witness was an equivocating flop. No witness denied that the described trip took place. No one even inferred that someone other than Wilkins had fired the death shots. No expert contradicted the FBI's ballistic tests. No one denied that Gene Thomas owned the murder weapon. Jack Nelson noted that the defense took a total of only twenty minutes ("Questions on Dixie Judicial System Raised by Klansman's Murder Trial," *Los Angeles Times*, May 9, 1965, D1). It was clear that Murphy's sole reliance would be on the trusted old Code of the South—the only "evidence" required was that the defendant was a klansman.

Klonsel Murphy thought that his closing argument would persuade at least one juror that a charged klansman deserved immunity in this murder case no matter what the state law says. Unfortunately, the official transcript does not contain the closing arguments. The practice in Alabama was to transcribe the witnesses' testimony, but not what was said by the lawyers in argument. However, much of the oral argument can be reconstituted from May 8, 1965 reports in both the national and local press, and *LIFE Magazine*'s May 21, 1965 articles containing portions of an unofficial transcript of Murphy's closing.[3]

The descriptions that follow are based on accounts published in the *Montgomery Advertiser*, the *New York Times*, the *Los Angeles Times*, and *LIFE Magazine*. Those accounts are fully consistent with the author's personal recollections.

On behalf of the state, Arthur Gamble calmly and carefully recounted the evidence that had been presented. He was brief and to the point, just as he had been in his opening statement. Gamble stressed that not often did the state have an eyewitness to a murder, but it did in this case. He recognized that some might be suspicious of the reports of a paid informer, but then he reviewed all of the evidence from state and federal sources confirming exactly what the eyewitness said. The evidence was overwhelming and, he said, the jury's duty was clear. He did not dwell on the victim or the reasons

---

3   On the second day of the trial, some enterprising reporter noted that the windows of the second-floor courtroom were always open, allowing spectators who gathered under a cool shade tree behind the courthouse to catch the louder bits of the proceedings in shady comfort. A truck arrived shortly thereafter and disgorged a large tripod that was connected to electronic equipment and placed under the shade tree. Mounted on the tripod was a directional microphone two or three feet long that was pointed directly at the open window. It apparently worked well enough to preserve much of Murphy's closing argument.

for her visit to Alabama. In fact, at one point he said that neither he nor the jury agreed with the purposes of her visit, thus proclaiming that Lowndes County was an insular segregated community that it is hard to believe ever existed in the middle of the twentieth century in the United States. Instead, he talked about the cold-blooded murder of a defenseless woman who just happened to be in Lowndes County. "But, gentlemen she was here, and she had a right to be here on our highways without getting shot down in the middle of the night," Gamble told the jury.

Gamble solemnly stated that "the decision you make in this case is going to be an historic one." He urged the jurors to be courageous for the sake of Lowndes County. His finish was best captured in Roy Reed's account ("Liuzzo Case Jury Retires for Night Without a Verdict," *New York Times*, May 7, 1965, 1, 25):

> The square-jawed solicitor, drawing himself to his full 6 feet 3 inches, urged the jury in a slow, commanding voice: "Don't put the stamp of approval on chaos, confusion and anarchy."
>
> Mr. Gamble pleaded, "Let's not let people like the defendant come into Lowndes County and drag us down from our high moral standards. If we blink at cold-blooded killing, we will turn this county over to chaos and confusion."
>
> Mr. Gamble said he realized that the murder had not involved residents of Lowndes County.
>
> "This has been forced on you and now we have got to deal with it the best we can," he said.

County Solicitor Carlton Perdue (who had joined Gamble in the prosecution) also made a short argument. He publicly addressed Murphy as "my dear friend" and his accompanying klansmen as these "gentlemen." To me, he looked for all the world as if he was swallowing a dose of distasteful medicine. Perdue asked "for a verdict that would say, 'murder must stop'" (Judith Helms, "Klansman's Fate In Hands of Jury," *Montgomery Advertiser*, May 7, 1965, 1).

Matt Murphy then rose, took center stage, and proceeded to address the all-white jury for over an hour in carefully coded language. He began speaking slowly in a calm voice. Murphy said he appeared there as "one white man to another," but quickly disclaimed any intention "to speak to your prejudices." He asked that if he had done anything "that met with your disapproval, don't blame that boy over there. Blame me." As reported in the *Los Angeles Times* (Nelson, May 9, 1965, 16):

> Then he launched into Rowe quoting Jesus Christ as saying, "What advantage is there if a man gain the whole world and then lose his soul?"
>
> "What kind of a man is Gary Tommy Rowe," he bellowed, "who comes into a fraternal organization—by hook or crook—cares not what he swears to—joins the United Klans for 30 pieces of silver."
>
> Murphy called the FBI informant "a treacherous rattlesnake and viper" and said he would accept money from Communists, the NAACP and Dr. Martin Luther King.

The klonsel then moved from Rowe to attack the FBI (Helms, May 7, 1965, 1):

> Murphy charged that Rowe was "drilled" by the FBI before he testified and that he appeared to be drugged or hypnotized.
>
> FBI Director J. Edgar Hoover and "his gang" also were attacked by Murphy, who said they "have run this case from beginning to end."
>
> "The FBI took this case away from your own white sheriff," the defense attorney told the 12 jurors.

Murphy returned again and again to Tommy Rowe, claiming that he could not be trusted and that he was part of an anti-klan conspiracy (Reed, May 7, 1965, 1, 25):

> But his chief defense was a scathing attack on the character and motives of the state's witness.
>
> He told the jury that Mr. Rowe had taken an oath of allegiance to the Ku Klux Klan and had violated it "for 30 pieces of silver."

"Remember Judas Iscariot, who took the high priests to Jesus Christ," Mr. Murphy said. "This man is a liar and a perjurer," he said. "How can you believe such a man, gentlemen?"

Mr. Murphy suggested that Mr. Rowe was part of a giant conspiracy to destroy the United Klans of America and the South, a conspiracy that included the FBI and President Johnson.

"He (Rowe) was paid to do it," the lawyer shouted, and then his voice trailed off in a bitter murmur, "money . . . silver . . . Judas Iscariot."

The *Los Angeles Times* reported that Murphy also assailed the FBI forensic expert in racial terms, ignoring the idea that science is a search for objective truth (Nelson, May 9, 1965):

"A crook who sits in Washington in the FBI crime lab," was Murphy's description of FBI Agent Marion Williams, who had identified a weapon seized at Thomas' home as the murder weapon.

Murphy drew laughter from some of the audience, especially a group of about 50 klansmen and their relatives when he said that Williams lived in Virginia because he didn't want his children "going to school with niggers in Washington."

The Klan attorney claimed to have shattered Williams expert testimony, but said that he had heard a gasp from the audience as he bore in on cross-examination of the agent: "What is that crazy lawyer doing?"

But, as captured in the *LIFE Magazine* excerpts, the Murphy closing dwelled on one recurring theme—race, race, race. Since *LIFE's* account stands alone as the virtual transcript of Matt Murphy's closing argument, it is set forth here at some length with the hope that it will prove how far we have come from the sorry state of racial affairs only fifty years ago (*LIFE*, May 31, 1965, 35):

"And this white woman who got killed? White woman? Where's that N.A.A.C.P. card? I thought I'd never see the day when Communists and niggers and Jews were flying under the banner of the United Nations flag, not the American flag we fought for. . . . I'm proud to be a white man and I'm proud that I stand up on my feet for white supremacy, not the mixing and the mongrelization of races . . . not the Zionists that run that bunch of niggers. The white people are not gonna run before them. And when white people join up to 'em they become white niggers.

"Do you know those big black niggers were driven by the woman, sitting in the back seat? Niggers! One white woman and these niggers. Right there. Riding right through your county. Communists dominate them niggers. . . .

"You know what that nigger [Leroy Moton] said on the stand. No. Yeah. No. Yeah. Like a 10-year-old boy. He should have been saying Yes, sir and No, sir before that honorable white judge. But the buck hasn't got the sense, the morals or the decency.

"I said now look, boy. Look down at your feet. Niggers only understand this kind of talk. How many feets away was that car? So he looked down at his feet and said about 25 feet away. . . . He said he passed out for 25–30 minutes. . . . What's he doing down there all that time? In that car alone with that woman.

"Then the nigger ran up the road and a truck came by and he stopped it. There was a rabbi in that truck. A rabbi. Of course, he stopped and put the nigger in the back. And there they were—rabbi with a nigger . . . white woman, nigger man, nigger woman—all in there, feet to feet.

"Integration breaks every moral law God ever wrote. Noah's son was Ham and he committed adultery and was banished and his sons were Hamites and God banished them and they went to Africa and the only thing they ever built was grass huts. No white woman can ever marry a descendant of Ham. That's God's law. . . . I don't care what Lyndon Johnson or anybody else says."

It was quite a study in contrast when Alabama Assistant Attorney General Joe Breck Gantt stood up to make the state's rebuttal argument for the prosecution. On three occasions during his closing, Murphy had referred to Gantt as the personal representative of State Attorney General Richmond Flowers, who was widely reported to be soliciting black votes in a run for governor. Compared to Murphy, Gantt was very subdued, but he tried to make his message a forceful one without treading too close to the jurors' racial sensitivities.

The *New York Times* reported that Gantt began with a kind of plea on behalf of the southern domestic servants and their employers (Reed, May 7, 1965):

> "If we are going to justify a cold-blooded murder, then it has to be done on the ground that this woman was riding in a car with a Negro man, and that this woman was down here where she had no business.
>
> If those are going to be the grounds for justifying murder in Lowndes County today, then tomorrow it may be grounds for a murder if someone of the temperament of the defendant here sees you driving your Negro maid home, or sees your wife driving her cook home."
>
> Mr. Gantt reminded the jury that Gov. George C. Wallace had called Mrs. Liuzzo's murder "a cowardly act that should not go unpunished."
>
> He said he doubted that even the officers of the Ku Klux Klan were unashamed of "this murder of a defenseless woman."
>
> Mr. Gantt asked, "Is this what our forefathers fought for in the Civil War— this kind of 'bravery,' the kind that it takes to shoot down a defenseless woman?"

It was around three o'clock on Thursday, May 6 when the arguments ended and the case was ready to go to the jury. The trial had lasted less than three days after the jury was empaneled.

The judge read the jury his legal instructions in a low, steady monotone that could likely put almost anyone to sleep and, at 3:45 p.m., the jury retired to consider its verdict. At 5:00 p.m., the jurors asked for more instructions. The foreman, the same person who earlier had raised questions in open court, now asked if they were limited to first-degree murder or "are we free to select a lesser charge?" At this, a woman spectator sitting near me gasped, "My God, I can't believe it, they are going to convict!" The judge repeated his earlier charge, that they could choose among murder in the first degree, murder in the second degree, or first-degree manslaughter. At 8:00 p.m., the judge excused them for the night.

On Friday morning, the jury asked again about the different offenses, and about the instruction on accomplices (Alabama allows no conviction on the uncorroborated testimony of an accomplice). At 1:00 p.m. they reported they were "locked tight," but the judge directed them to continue to try. On May 7, 1965, at 4:05 p.m., the twelve white men on the jury reported that they were still hopelessly deadlocked, standing ten to two for conviction. Bubba Gamble had fallen short of any conviction for any charge by two votes (Roy Reed, "A Mistrial in Liuzzo Case; Jury 10–2 For Conviction," *New York Times*, May 8, 1965, 1, 15).

Murphy's racist antics and the Code of the South had hung another jury.

Chapter 10

HAYNEVILLE'S LONG, HOT SUMMER AND THE SECOND STATE TRIAL

"Reality is kaleidoscopic in the Black Belt . . . death in the midst of life, life in the midst of death," Jonathan M. Daniels wrote last April, in an essay printed in the Episcopal Theological School Journal.

Twenty-six years old and a second-year student on leave from studies at the Cambridge, Massachusetts seminary, the young man was describing his experience as a civil rights worker in Lowndes County, Alabama, where he went after a march from Selma to Montgomery to provide "a ministry of presence."

Poetic Prophecy—*Daniels' words were prophetic, for "death in the midst of life" came with bitter directness when he was shot to death a few months later in Hayneville, Alabama.*

—THE EPISCOPALIAN, OCTOBER 1965

The result of the first Collie Leroy Wilkins trial was covered extensively by media in the United States and abroad, and there was plenty of action in the aftermath. Alabama Attorney General Richmond Flowers immediately announced that there would be a retrial at the next term of the Lowndes County court in September 1965. Matt Murphy instantly began crowing that the ten guilty votes were most likely for "assault and battery." He predicted there would be a total acquittal next time around. Dr. King was pessimistic about a second trial: "I don't think any of these men will ever be convicted" (Roy Reed, "Dr. King Returns to Alabama Drive," *New York Times,* May 11, 1965, 25).

Newsmen searched for, found, and interviewed the two dissenting jurors, who turned out to be segregationists, "one a White Citizens' Counsel member and the other a former member" (Nelson, May 9, 1965, 16). These two holdouts said they were persuaded by the klan oath argument. Juror Billy Cheatham, a bookkeeper, didn't accept Rowe's testimony, "[n]ot after he swore before God and then broke his oath." The other holdout, Dan Lee, seemed to echo Cheatham's view: "Me and him are pretty much on the same side." The jury had quickly decided against either first or second degree murder and had voted on the remaining charge, first-degree manslaughter (Jack Nelson, "Mistrial Ruled in Liuzzo Case," *Los Angeles Times*, May 8, 1965, 1).[1]

At least some of the jurors in the majority said they had been turned off by Murphy's racist tactics; in the words of juror Edmund Sallee, "I think a great many of us were insulted to a great extent and he must have thought we were very, very ignorant" (*LIFE Magazine*, May 21, 1965, 37).

Matt Murphy took his three clients on tour in the South. The Associated Press reported that they all attended klan rallies at Dunn and Sanford, North Carolina, the largest attended by 6,000 people. Defendant Wilkins signed autographs and Murphy spoke about how "[t]he NAACP . . . is actually ruled by an international Zionist Jewish movement which wants to take over the government." While klanswomen passed through the crowd collecting money, Murphy reassured the world that no white jury in Alabama would ever convict Wilkins.

The world did not stop while Alabama waited for the second trial. The burdens on the retrial in Lowndes County kept mounting higher and higher. A review of what went on in Lowndes County as the starting time got closer shows the chances of conviction were quickly falling to nearly absolute zero.

The publicity generated by the first trial gave a real boost to the drive to register black voters in Lowndes County. Stokely Carmichael (later known as Kwame Ture) of the Student Nonviolent Coordinating Committee, who seemed to stress black power rather than nonviolence, had started to organize Lowndes County in March 1965, but found it very hard to compete with the general focus on Selma. Now, to the dismay of the county's whites, Lowndes had become a major new focus of the civil rights movement, at-

---

1   In Alabama manslaughter is a Class B felony punishable by two to twenty years in prison (Alabama Criminal Code §§ 13A-6-3, 13A-5-6). It is an included lesser offense in a charge of first degree murder (Alabama Criminal Code § 13A-1-9).

tracting plenty of young volunteers from up north. The official ballot symbol Carmichael selected for the new Lowndes County Freedom Party was the black panther. Racial tension in Lowndes County grew steadily.

Meanwhile in Washington, and despite the predicable southern filibuster, Congress passed a tough new voting rights bill, which had been born in the outraged reaction of the country, and of President Johnson, to Selma on Bloody Sunday. On August 6, Congress passed the Voting Rights Act of 1965 and President Johnson signed it into law. Right after the bill was signed, Attorney General Katzenbach designated nine of the most resistant southern counties, and ordered federal examiners to open offices in them immediately. For the first time ever, federal officials had begun to conduct registration of blacks in the South. The Alabama counties in that first group designated under the Act included Selma's Dallas County and Bloody Lowndes. After nearly a century of playing litigation games over voter registration, the new system abruptly took over. First hundreds, then thousands, of blacks in the South began to register and vote.[2]

But the strain related to the voting rights campaign and federal registrars was soon augmented by even more serious events. On just one day, August 20, 1965, the grim reaper gave the Liuzzo murder retrial a double hit. First, an early morning car accident claimed the life of klan klonsel Matt Murphy, whose bumbling, racist flailing had almost given prosecutor Gamble a minor victory in the first trial. He would be replaced by a former Birmingham mayor, Arthur Hanes, a practicing attorney and a former FBI agent who would make no such mistakes.

Second, on the very same day, in broad daylight, just a half block from the Hayneville courthouse, Thomas L. Coleman, a member of one of Lowndes County's leading families, used his shotgun to kill Jonathan Daniels, a white seminarian. He also grievously wounded Richard Morrisroe, a Catholic priest. They had been part of a group of civil rights activists picketing Lowndes County stores in Port Deposit. They had all been arrested and jailed for disturbing the peace, but after several days in jail, they were released in Hayneville without prior notice. While waiting for their rides,

---

2   See Landsberg, *Enforcing Civil Rights*.

four of those released, three black and one white, went into Varner's Cash Store, a small convenience store, to buy sodas. Coleman shot Daniels as the seminarian was leaving the store.

Coleman right away admitted that he did the shooting, advancing a vague claim of defending the female owner from soda pop thievery. The State quickly appointed a special investigator and Attorney General Flowers exercised his statutory authority to take over this prosecution. When the Lowndes County Grand Jury returned a charge of manslaughter rather than murder, Flowers roundly and publicly scolded the jurors. Apparently anxious to get this Coleman matter out of the way, Judge Thagard then set a trial to begin September 27, thus deferring the Liuzzo murder retrial, which had been set for that same date.

Then the nationwide focus on Lowndes County juries quickly mushroomed. On August 25, in federal court in Montgomery, the American Civil Liberties Union (ACLU) filed suit on behalf of Lowndes County blacks, claiming that the county's jury selection system that excluded all women and blacks from serving as jurors was unconstitutional. The requested relief was to discontinue all jury trials in the county until it had a lawful jury selection system.

The public heat really turned up when Judge Thagard denied a motion made by the Alabama Attorney General to postpone the Coleman trial until the wounded priest, Father Morrisroe, who was recuperating in Chicago, had recovered enough to be able to return to Hayneville and testify. Thagard quickly ruled that the Alabama legislature had ensured that criminal defendants were entitled to a "speedy trial," and suggested that perhaps the prosecution could just read the priest's sworn statement to the jury.

When Assistant Attorney General Joe Breck Gantt persisted and finally flatly refused to go to trial without testimony from his main eyewitness to the crime, Judge Thagard ruled that Gantt and Attorney General Flowers could no longer participate as prosecutors in this case. Instead, he ordered Circuit Solicitor Gamble and County Solicitor Perdue to take over the prosecution and begin a "speedy trial" beginning on September 28, only thirty-nine days after the shootings. No explanation was offered as to why the Coleman trial could not have been postponed until after the scheduled murder retrial of Wilkins.

Coleman's "speedy trial" began on September 28 and went to the jury on the 29th. The jury deliberated a total of ninety minutes before returning an acquittal, and, without even taking the witness stand, Tom Coleman found himself a free man. The twelve white male jurors in this case accepted the defense that Coleman had been called to the scene to protect the little lady who ran the Varner's Cash Store where the victims, waiting for their rides, had gone to purchase sodas. Coleman got a call while playing dominoes at the Hayneville Courthouse. His buddies testified that both the priest and the seminarian, who had just been released from county custody a few hours before the shootings, were carrying weapons—a gun and a knife, respectively—and that each of them had "menaced" Coleman with those weapons. Of course, his only recourse was to shoot both of them with a shotgun he had happened to pick up and was carrying with him.[3]

Coleman's alert friends also testified that some unidentified black men then came and took the missing weapons from the priest and seminarian, before running away, never to be seen again. The fifty-three-minute defense included good-character testimony from the sheriff of Butler County, two probate judges, and two ministers. The very good news verdict was announced by Coleman's cousin, court clerk Kelly Coleman (not to be confused with his sister, the county's superintendent of education, who would soon be a named defendant in a local school desegregation case).

The cries of outrage that were now directed at Lowndes County from across Alabama and America made the public anguish over the first Liuzzo verdict pale by comparison. Bloody Lowndes had reverted to type. For Cole-

---

3   The Justice Department asked the FBI to investigate this killing for possible prosecution under 18 U.SC §242—Deprivation of rights under color of law. The Bureau reported that while Coleman carried identification as a deputy sheriff, he was neither employed by nor authorized to work as part of any law enforcement agency in Hayneville. Instead, it was a local custom for the sheriff to provide "deputy cards" to authorize those who wished to purchase and carry firearms in the county. Although Coleman has been described in news stories as a "Deputy Sheriff" or a "Special Deputy," in fact he had no such status. Thus he did not fire his personal shotgun while acting under "color of law" and could not be prosecuted under 18 USC § 242.

man, there had been no real trial, and for Daniels and Morrisroe no justice at all.

Richmond Flowers, a gubernatorial candidate and then Alabama Attorney General, announced publicly that this acquittal represented the "democratic process going down the drain of irrationality, bigotry and improper enforcement of the law." He warned that "those who feel they have [to have] a license to kill, destroy and cripple have been issued that license." Within days, Flowers announced that his office was taking over the second trial of Wilkins in the Liuzzo killing and would do everything possible to get a fair jury (Roy Reed, "Liuzzo Case Gets New Prosecutor," *New York Times*, October 17, 1965, 1).

At the height of the national furor over Judge Thagard's refusal to delay the Coleman trial, I was in our Selma office on other business when I got a call from Gamble saying that Judge Thagard would like to see me in his chambers in Hayneville. While I had met the judge during the first trial, we had only a courteous, arm's-length relationship. I was somewhat surprised at his request and I checked with Assistant Attorney General Doar in Washington before agreeing to go to the meeting.

In his chambers, Judge Thagard greeted me in an extremely gracious manner. After commenting on the pleasant weather, he said he had asked me to come in so that he could pass on something directly to me and to my associates in the Justice Department. He wanted to offer his personal assurance that he had made his speedy trial ruling in the Coleman matter strictly in accordance with Alabama law. In fact, he described in some detail how he spent hours researching and studying the law books, trying to find some other, some different resolution, because he knew it would appear to some that Coleman might be getting a "hometown deal." But he said he truly believed that Alabama law required him to hold a speedy trial and he could not postpone it indefinitely. "Some far-off witness recovering from a serious wound was not subject to the court's subpoena power and might never agree to come to Alabama to testify," he explained. He described this as the "hardest call" he had made in all his years on the bench.

I was taken aback and muttered something neutral about seeing that his message was relayed. He continued, for the first time calling me by name:

"Jim, please tell them that I have done my very best to do this job in the right way. I can't tell you how hard it is waking up in the morning knowing that all over the country, hundreds of thousands of people are thinking you are a son of a bitch." I could only respond that, being unfamiliar with Alabama law, I was in no position to comment, other than to say that the public was concerned also with the appearance of fairness. I called Doar in Washington and relayed the message, but was told only to advise the judge that it had been delivered.

On October 1, even though its jury case had yet to be heard, the ACLU presented a seldom, if ever, granted emergency motion to the U.S. Supreme Court asking that no further jury trials be held in Lowndes County until a fair system was in place. Justice Hugo Black predictably denied this emergency motion without opinion. Reporters interviewed the recovering priest in Chicago who again denied carrying any weapon after being released from jail in Hayneville. Civil rights groups, editorial writers, and newspaper cartoonists roundly condemned this latest example of the miscarriage of justice in Bloody Lowndes.

Thus, in October 1965 the second Liuzzo trial began in a totally poisoned atmosphere. The first trial had come close to a misdemeanor conviction only because of the racist bumbling of defense counsel Matt Murphy and the trust the local jurors had in their local prosecutor. Now Murphy was gone and steady Bubba Gamble had been replaced as prosecutor by a flamboyant racial moderate, Richmond Flowers, who was despised by Lowndes County's whites. On the political trail, Flowers was now openly pitching new black voters to help him replace George Wallace as governor, and he had publicly ridiculed the Lowndes County jury system.[4]

Flowers and Gantt went right to work trying to demonstrate the bias of the Lowndes County jury system. Unlike the first trial, where the judge asked qualifying questions to batches of ten prospective jurors, the new prosecution team insisted on examining each one individually. Initially, forty men were called. Probably because of the ACLU's jury case and the federally

---

4   In fact, even as the retrial began, other Justice Department lawyers in Washington were studying whether to join the ACLU's lawsuit attacking the county's jury selection system.

supervised voter registration in Lowndes County, there were, for the first time ever, seven black men included in the jury pool (Roy Reed, "2nd Liuzzo Trial Will Open Today: Prosecution Will Challenge Jury System in South," *New York Times*, October 18, 1965, 24).

The prosecutors asked each white if they believed white people were inherently superior to blacks, and if they were members of the klan or the white citizens' council. Each black was asked if he had ever been called to serve in the past. None had. Several blacks said they opposed the death penalty and a couple said they had formed "fixed impressions" about the case. The final array from which twelve jurors would be selected was twenty-eight whites and two blacks. The bottom line would be the same as always: the Lowndes County jury box would be filled with all white males.

The new prosecutors asked the judge to disqualify for cause eleven white prospects who said that they believed that white civil rights workers were "inferior." In a case where the murder victim was exactly such a person, their argument was that including eleven such persons in the array of prospective jurors would or could deprive the state of a fair trial. Judge Thagard firmly refused to disqualify such persons—or even klansmen. In fact, when Flowers moved to strike for cause the only prospect who admitted to having a klan background, the judge recalled the man and invited him to say that he could try the case fairly.[5] The judge then ruled that all were legally qualified and if the prosecutors did not want them to serve they could excuse them when the sides struck the jurors until only twelve remained (Roy Reed, "Liuzzo Panel Men Declare Racism: 25 of 32 Examined for Jury Back White Supremacy," *New York Times*, October 19, 1965, 29).

For me, dealing with Richmond Flowers was entirely different from providing federal witnesses and evidence to prosecutor Gamble. Gamble's strategy had been to convince the jurors to punish the irresponsible klansmen from upstate who had brought trouble and shame to Lowndes County. Flowers, on the other hand, thought there was now no way to convict with a deeply biased jury. He said he was determined to expose the Lowndes

---

5   Alabama's unique "struck jury" is explained in chapter 5, p. 31, note 8.

County legal process as a sham and a farce. This would highlight the need for jury reform while advancing his own political agenda for the gubernatorial election.

After the first day of examining potential jurors, Flowers and Gantt came to my hotel room in Montgomery. They fretted about how the prosecution had no chance in a closed society such as Lowndes County. The jurors all tended to share the same biased views, and there was nothing they could do about it. In the course of the conversation, I mentioned that in really extraordinary circumstances, when a trial judge refused to apply the law fairly, I had heard of prosecutors sometimes asking to suspend the trial while they sought emergency relief from an appellate court. I made it clear that this was only a kind of last-ditch possibility that, if consistent with Alabama law, might be applied in a jury selection issue. Flowers thought for about thirty seconds and then pronounced that this was a great approach and that he would do it. He said he knew it would never work, but that it would show the world how he was pulling out all the stops.

The next day, the prosecutors again asked Judge Thagard to disqualify the eleven prospective jurors who had been critical of civil rights workers. When the judge again refused, Flowers requested a twenty-four-hour delay so that the issue could be presented to the Alabama Supreme Court on an extraordinary writ. To the amazement of all of us, Judge Thagard granted this request (Roy Reed, "Liuzzo Prosecutor Asks Juror Purge," *New York Times*, October 20, 1965, 1).

The trial court proceedings stopped for a day and a half, while a motion for such relief was hastily put together and promptly denied (Roy Reed, "White Supremacist Jurors Approved in Liuzzo Case," *New York Times*, October 21, 1965, 1). Newspapers and television, in and out of Alabama, carried images of the tight-lipped, crusading State Attorney General fighting for a fair jury in a race case. In future brainstorming sessions I was much more guarded in offering suggestions.

The evidence and testimony in the second trial was much as it had been in the first, but was presented without the racist theatrics of Matt Murphy. Assistant Attorney General Joe Breck Gantt examined almost all the witnesses in a serious, very low key manner. Defense counsel Hanes neither blustered nor used racial slurs (Roy Reed, "Rowe Again Tells of Liuzzo Killing," *New York Times*, October 22, 1965, 28).

Each night, Richmond Flowers would knock on my door to discuss that day's events and to try out the closing argument he was drafting. Now he had conceived of a dramatic closing that would not only attract public attention, but might even contain a slim chance of convincing—even shaming—the jurors into voting for conviction. As he originally proposed it, the climax of his peroration would focus on the Holy Bible. In a stern tone, he would read from the Ten Commandments, "Thou shalt not kill." He acted out for me how he would then advance toward the jury box holding a Bible and pronounce loudly and dramatically that if the jury did not hold this defendant accountable, they might as well "tare da page outta' da book and tro' it on da flo" (vernacular for "tear the page out of the book and throw it on the floor"). Whereupon, he would rip out the text containing this commandment from the Bible, crumple it up, and dramatically cast it onto the floor at the jurors' feet. I certainly did not advise him to do this, but did acknowledge that it could be a "powerful" message.

Even though most of white Lowndes disliked Attorney General Flowers, the prospect of hearing the lawyers argue this important case was a drawing card that filled the entire courtroom with spectators. A lady in front of me explained to her friends that she hadn't paid any attention to this case, but was there because she "just loved" to hear the lawyers argue, "even that no-good Richmond Flowers."

As he told me afterward, Flowers decided against using a real Bible in his final plea for justice. At the last minute, members of his staff had persuaded him that, in a Bible Belt state like Alabama, publicly mutilating a "Holy Book" could risk offending too many people. Instead, while retaining the forceful image of discarding the rules, he settled on a rather pallid substitute for the Good Book—Black's Law Dictionary.

Even in its modified state, Roy Reed did credit him with a dramatic closing ("Klansman Freed in Liuzzo Killing," *New York Times*, October 23, 1965, 1):

State Attorney General Richmond M. Flowers . . . told the jury in a fiery summation:

"If you do not convict this man, you might as well lock up the courthouse, open up the jail and throw away the keys. And, you can take true verdict and just tear it out of the book and throw it away, because it won't mean a thing."

As he shouted the words, he ripped several pages from Black's Law Dictionary—the section defining "true verdict"—and hurled them to the floor causing a stir in the packed courtroom.

"In 15 months you will have another Attorney General and I will be just history." A low chorus of "amens" came from the audience.

"But I want to tell you this, gentlemen," he said. "The blood of this man's sin, if you do not find him guilty, will stain the very soul of our county for an eternity."

The courtroom was hushed as the tall, red-haired lawyer finished and sat down.

In his closing, defense counsel Hanes attacked Rowe's credibility with a clever wordplay rather than the unvarnished scorn used previously by Matt Murphy. Comparing Rowe to the animal that legend says is trained to lead others to their slaughter, the *Montgomery Advertiser* reported that Hanes called the trial "the parable of two goats—a Judas-goat and a scape-goat."

The sadly predictable result was not long in coming (Reed, October 23, 1965):

An all-white jury today found Collie Leroy Wilkins, Jr., a 22-year-old Ku Klux Klansman, not guilty of the murder of Mrs. Viola Gregg Liuzzo.

The verdict came after 1 hour and 35 minutes of deliberation. Several spectators in the courtroom, which was filled with white people, burst into applause when the verdict was read.

On October 23, 1965, it took these white jurors, whose souls had been probed so relentlessly by the passionate state attorney general, only about an hour and a half to find the defendant not guilty. It became a perverse study in equal southern justice because that was precisely how long it had taken another "Bloody Lowndes" jury to acquit Tom Coleman of manslaughter just three weeks earlier. In fact, all the political grandstanding by Richmond Flowers had made things worse now, producing not a hung jury, but an outright acquittal of the klansman whose shots had killed Mrs. Liuzzo.[6]

Two days later, on October 25, 1965, the Justice Department announced it would seek to reform the Lowndes County jury system by joining the ACLU's pending lawsuit.

---

6   In his authorized biography, Flowers' recollection of these trials is seriously flawed (John Hayman, *Bitter Harvest: Richmond Flowers and the Civil Rights Revolution* [Montgomery, Alabama: Black Belt Press, 1996], 227–29). Describing the first Wilkins murder trial, for example, Flowers is quoted as saying that "[t]he district attorney didn't do one thing in the world, so Joe [Breck Gantt] had to try the entire case." In fact, as related above (chapters 5–9), the transcript of that case shows just the opposite: Gantt actually examined only one witness, while Gamble did all the rest. As to the second trial, Flowers remembered that "[t]he district attorney said he wasn't going to try it again . . . because he couldn't get a verdict. That's when I came in. He'll tell you now that he was going to prosecute and I was just grandstanding and pushed him out of the way." The author's own memory and every single contemporary account reflects that Flowers used his statutory authority as Attorney General to remove Gamble and take over this local prosecution. Flowers also remembers that there were some blacks on the second jury, but the official transcript and every media account confirm that all the jurors were white.

Chapter 11

THE FEDERAL TRIAL

I have a dream that one day the state of Alabama, whose governor's lips are presently dripping with the words of interposition and nullification, will be transformed into a situation where little black boys and black girls will be able to join hands with little white boys and white girls and walk together as sisters and brothers.

— DR. MARTIN LUTHER KING, JR., "I HAVE A DREAM," ADDRESS AT THE LINCOLN MEMORIAL, WASHINGTON, DC, AUGUST 28, 1963

Even though Alabama Attorney General Richmond Flowers publicly announced the State's intent to proceed with the murder trials of Eugene Thomas and William Eaton, the U.S. Justice Department decided that the time had come to try its federal conspiracy case against all three klansmen. It was November of 1965 and now the state had twice failed to convict the killer of Viola Liuzzo, who was shot for attending a demonstration that had been approved in advance by a federal court. The time had arrived for the federal government to try to deliver some measure of justice with its federal conspiracy indictment.

On the surface, it was not at all clear that the Justice Department's chance of a conviction was significantly better than the State of Alabama's had been. There was the unavoidable problem of the klan's clandestine alliance with Alabama jurors, the complexities of the federal conspiracy law so rarely used in the past hundred years, and now a state verdict that had acquitted one of the klansmen of any homicide even manslaughter.

Still there would be some advantages in taking the case to the federal district court in Montgomery. First, there would be a fair trial, freed from the racial animosities that permeated Lowndes County. Also, this case had been assigned to Judge Frank Johnson, a renowned jurist who was well acquainted with much of the background. Indeed, it was his order that made it clear that the March to Montgomery to petition for the right to vote was legal and proper, and the indictment of the klansmen charged that his order had defined the very rights that the klan conspiracy had taken away. Johnson ran a tight ship and had a reputation of compelling strict compliance with the Constitution and federal law in civil rights cases. This trial would not be encumbered by any Matt Murphy-type shenanigans; Johnson would not tolerate them.[1]

Second, a federal jury, which could include both women and blacks, would be much more fair and objective. It would also be drawn from a much larger pool of jurors. The evidence we were helping to generate for the jury discrimination case showed that in tiny Lowndes County the entire population of white males over twenty-one was only 889, and the practice had been to use only a fraction of those. In a recent twelve-year period in Lowndes County jury cases, a miniscule nucleus of only 211 white males had accounted for two-thirds of all the people called to serve on juries. In contrast, Judge Johnson would be drawing multiracial male and female jurors at random from the many thousands of eligible people in twelve counties, including some of the state's most populous cities.[2]

Finally, the prosecutors would have very expansive resources. For general investigative and forensic support they could call on the resources of the FBI. For legal resources they looked to a committed group of lawyers and professionals in the Justice Department's Civil Rights Division, ably led by

---

1 See photo 17.

2 The 1965 Liuzzo federal trial was before an all-white, all-male jury. While some women were included in federal jury pools in the state, Alabama prohibited all female jury service until the Civil Rights Act of 1957 was enacted. But in 1965 the number of potential female jurors in Alabama, even in federal courts, was still quite small. Adding a few blacks and women to a large jury pool did not guarantee that members either group would actually sit on a federal jury. The first female juror to sit in an Alabama State Court was selected in 1966. Federal law now requires all juries to be fairly representative and does not allow peremptory challenges to be used on the basis of race or gender. See Carter v. Jury Comm'n, 396 U. S. 320, 396 U. S. 330 (1970); Taylor v. Louisiana, 419 U.S. 522 (1975); Batson v. Kentucky, 476 U.S. 79 (1986); J.E.B. v. Alabama ex rel T.B., 511 U.S. 127 (1994); Miller-El v. Dretke, 545 U.S. 231 (2005).

Assistant Attorney General Doar, a fearless civil rights advocate. The Division had become expert at forming a team to support the trial of big cases. For local credibility, they could count on the participation of Ben Hardeman, the U.S. attorney for the Middle District of Alabama, whose office was highly respected for its enforcement of all federal laws, from bank robbery to draft dodging.

Institutionally, the Civil Rights Division's approach was to go all out to win tough cases and to do so by out-lawyering its opponents. Created by the Civil Rights Act of 1957, from the very first, the Division's assignments were challenging: to bring locally unpopular cases to enforce black voting rights in the South and to continue the pioneer prosecution work of the Civil Rights Section of the Criminal Division of the Justice Department. During the days of President Franklin Roosevelt's New Deal a small cadre of lawyers in the Criminal Division had virtually disinterred the Reconstruction era anti-klan laws (18 U.S.C. §§ 241 and 242), which had been designed to end klan violence. This small group had been successful in using these old laws and then kept them alive with a dogged series of carefully chosen prosecutions until the Supreme Court finally confirmed their continued validity. Now, in the dawning light of general civil rights reform, enforcing that historic legislation would be the vehicle for bringing justice to the modern-day victims of klan terror crimes.

John Doar, a Wisconsin Republican who had joined the Civil Rights Division near the end of the Eisenhower administration, soon became indispensable to Burke Marshall, President Kennedy's leader of the Division. Never a bureaucrat who would try to lead by poking pins in a map in Washington, Doar always went where the action was. He represented the Justice Department at the Freedom Rides and the integration of the University of Mississippi.[3]

---

3   Doar died on November, 11, 2014. His conduct in office made for a stellar record. He received the Presidential Medal of Freedom from President Obama in 2012. In his work for the Division, he personally prevented rioting in Jackson, Mississippi, when NAACP leader Medgar Evers was killed in 1963, personally argued major school desegregation cases, and successfully prosecuted the Liuzzo and the "Mississippi Burning" murder cases; the latter involved the murder of three civil rights workers in 1964. The conviction in the Liuzzo case came on his birthday. After leaving Justice, he came back to government to serve as special counsel to

During James Meredith's first few weeks at 'Ol Miss, Doar sent a Civil Rights Division lawyer to actually live with Meredith in his dorm room. Doar also conceived of the fact-intensive method of proving discrimination in voting. This involved having the FBI photocopy all of a county's voting records and conducting a painstaking analysis of how blacks had been treated differently from whites. He then insisted that sometimes hostile federal judges either face those facts or be reversed by the Court of Appeals for the Fifth Circuit in New Orleans.

Doar's concept was that the Division should function like a law firm where the most senior partners would handle the most significant cases. When it was time to try the Liuzzo klan conspiracy case, he put himself in charge and asked U.S. Attorney Hardeman and his assistant, J. O. Sentelle, to assist him in the courtroom. The Division's support group, operating completely out of public view, was headed by Doar's main man and my boss, D. Robert Owen, a Texan by way of Princeton. Bob's energy and no-stone-unturned commitment was legendary in the Division.[4]

The function of Owen's "boiler room" was to organize and package the Division's case. High-energy college graduates, mostly women with the title of Research Analyst, handled much of the heavy lifting. They read and summarized every FBI report on this or any potentially related investigation, prepared documentary exhibits, put together witness folders, made multiple copies of virtually everything, and in their spare time ran out for food and coffee for everyone else. Hiring these analysts, the precursors of modern-day paralegals, was another Doar innovation.[5]

A lawyer on Owen's team would be assigned to interview every potential witness, carefully reviewing with them any previous testimony, parsing their statements made to the FBI and others, and making a fresh and frank assess-

---

the House Judiciary Committee and personally presented the evidence (processed in a Doar boiler room) that led to bipartisan votes to impeach President Nixon in 1974. See photo 18.

4 See photo 19.

5 There is also a history of these analysts morphing into lawyers and yet another of a number of marriages between analysts and Division lawyers. Without going all through that history, it should suffice to say that the author's wife of forty years is one who went from Division analyst, to lawyer, to marriage.

ment of their strengths and weaknesses. Secretaries typed their notes on locally rented typewriters. Other lawyers proposed and argued about the most effective presentation of proof, producing the suggested order of witnesses.[6]

I was learning that the way the Civil Rights Division comprehensively prepared for trial was the secret of its success. Never lose a case that could be won with better preparation. Use the vast resources of the federal government to literally outwork the other side. Discover and win by getting absolutely ready to prove the absolute truth.

I was very proud when Doar invited me to go with him and to meet Judge Johnson in chambers for about three minutes before the trial began. Doar explained how I had attended the state trials and would be in the federal courtroom to assist in this trial. There was not much more to the meeting, except that I became an instant admirer of Judge Johnson and felt truly honored to have even a minor role in this prosecution.

The final product of all this frenzied effort was a calm, smooth presentation with no public semblance of overpreparation. We always joked that the lawyers presenting the case in the courtroom had the easiest job of all—just follow the script. With what our staff provided, a high school debater could have put on a winning case. Success came from the details of preparation, what Doar once dubbed "the romance of the records." For each witness, the presenter was handed a trial folder containing a detailed outline of the examination. Its facing page contained a checklist of items of information to be elicited from that witness with a space to check as it was covered. If the witness was to introduce or refer to exhibits, the exhibit would be included on the list with reference to its proposed identification number. The original of each documentary exhibit was in this folder, with copies for the court and the defense counsel. When the judge accepted an exhibit into evidence, the presenter made a check mark in the file, and the waiting trial team would

---

6   To the best of my memory the Liuzzo trial team directed by Bob Owen included the following Division lawyers and research analysts: Frank Allen, Frank Dunbaugh, Patsy Gessell, Brian Landsberg, Terry Lenzner, Maureen Murphy (Rayborn), Chad Quaintance, George Rayborn, Margaret Rood (Lenzner), John Rosenberg, Dorothy Shelton (Landsberg), Jean Voelker (Rosenberg), and Ray Terry. My apologies for any errors or omissions.

add that exhibit's number to its master list of admitted exhibits so that none were inadvertently omitted.

I was the new guy in this routine, but because I had lived through the state trials of the Liuzzo case Doar asked me to sit inside the bar of the court (but not at the counsel table) to perform several functions. I made a final review of each witness folder before handing it to the front men and made trial notes of everything that happened (in case there was an appeal before a transcript could be prepared). I also followed the details of the trial from an extra copy of the witness folder, as a final check, before a witness was excused, that every single item had been covered and every exhibit introduced. If I spotted something, **anything of note,** I was to write and hand a message to one of our principals.

Above all, with Doar in charge there would never be any public criticism of the copious federal resources devoted to the case. No federal judge or jury would ever see someone from the Owen team or a gaggle of curious FBI agents just lolling around among the courtroom spectators. That would cause internal "demerits" that reflected badly on your professionalism and performance. These rules were absolute and serious. During one break, Doar tersely mentioned that he had seen me just "watching" instead of busily taking notes.

There was no possible comparison between this and the way the Liuzzo murder case had been tried in the state court in Hayneville. Judge Johnson was an absolute bear on judicial decorum and diligence; Judge Thagard let anything go and just barely kept the case moving. Johnson's court was only thirty miles, but it seemed like thirty light years, from the casual atmosphere in Hayneville, with its courtroom cage, its illegally segregated restrooms, and its noisy klansmen swaggering around the defense table chatting and smoking cigarettes.

Doar's opening statement clearly set out the elements of the conspiracy and how the government expected to prove each one. The two eyewitnesses and the federal witnesses each delivered a clear and believable story in a straightforward way. The government's case went solidly and completely with only one or two problems along the way. We all felt good about it.

The defense was able to make a few points, but nothing that threatened our basic case. The focus was on Rowe and his credibility. Defense counsel Hanes did introduce a picture of several klansmen, pointing out one who looked like Rowe, all hovering over a downed freedom rider in Birmingham in 1961. Rowe denied that it was him in the picture, but there was no way to resolve the issue in court. He also denied it when we interviewed him. The jury would have to figure it out.

The biggest gaffe by defense counsel Hanes came when cross-examining Special Agent Shanahan, who testified prior to Rowe. In pursuing a specific point, Hanes asked what Rowe had told Shanahan on that subject in their conversation after the killing. Since the defense had thus "opened the door" by asking about this conversation, Doar, on redirect, was now able to have this professional FBI witness relate everything else that Rowe had told him the night of the shooting. All of this hearsay, which would normally be excluded, could be introduced on the record because of the defense counsel's question about Shanahan's conversation with Rowe. Thus, the prosecution was able to present Rowe's account twice, once through the mouth of Shanahan, an experienced and likeable witness, and then again through Rowe's own testimony.

Unlike the state transcript, the federal reporter did transcribe the closing arguments. John Doar opened for the prosecution, Arthur Hanes argued for the defendants, and U.S. Attorney Ben Hardeman closed. There were no surprises and very little bombast. There are almost as many styles of closing arguments as there are lawyers who make them. This jury saw three competent but widely contrasting approaches.

This was the first time I saw Doar argue to a jury. He immediately struck me with his presence before the jury. He did not raise his voice, but spoke just loudly enough for all of them to hear. His manner was straightforward, and he maintained eye contact with the jurors throughout. His argument lasted only about fifteen minutes, but was very powerful in its simplicity. He offered no excess drama or any false sympathy with the juror's plight. Politely but firmly, Doar insisted that the jurors must deal with the terrible facts of what had actually happened out on Route 80 that night.

He began by saying that the jurors knew this was an important case and he was sure they would decide it solely on the basis of "the evidence you heard in this court room, and based upon the court's instructions." He then went through the evidence, point by point, reminding the jurors of each item of evidence and how forensic exhibits confirmed the elements of Rowe's story. "Everything that Tommy Rowe told the F.B.I. within three and a half hours after this crime occurred proved out to be the fact," he told the jury. He went on that there was no "doubt who did this, who killed Mrs. Liuzzo, so the next question is why did they do this?"

They did it, he stated plainly, as members of the klan, "because they were dedicated members of an organization . . . dedicated to preserving segregation by any lawful or unlawful means." He reviewed the evidence of what the defendants did and said that day that made it clear to anyone that they had made this trip to interfere with and deny the rights set forth in the court order, the right to march to Montgomery and present grievances to the Governor. He concluded that this certainly was not a close case that required much careful balancing. All the right was one side, the side of the demonstrators:

> As I say, the rights were all on the side of these people, all of them; not just a few of them, not the ones that you happen to like, not the ones you happen to dislike, not the ones you happen to hate, not the ones you happen to despise, but . . . all of them, and they came from our system of law, and there just isn't any doubt about it.

Defense counsel Hanes job was much different and so was his approach. He first sowed the seed that the jury had the power to bring its own values to bear. A jury was not like a computer in which one could insert all the evidence and "push a button, the lights would come on, and the bells would ring, and out would come a true verdict." That, he told them, cannot be done; there is "no replacement for the human mind, and the heart."

Hanes then read the indictment that detailed the charges against the defendants and listed the "rights" that they had allegedly violated. He proceeded to dissect the actions that the defendants had taken and argued that each act was perfectly legal. On March 21, they had participated in a klan protest of Judge Johnson's order permitting the civil rights march. "So they had a little motorcade—lasted about twenty minutes, and it broke up. Nothing illegal or wrong about it." On March 25, they drove to Montgomery, parked, and walked to a filling station. "Was there anything wrong with that? Not a thing." He proceeded through the day's various stops, making the same point about each one, that it was a perfectly legal action.

So, nothing the defendants did that day was illegal, unless one accepts the story of the informant, Tommy Rowe. But is Rowe, a professional snitch, worthy of belief? Hanes reached over and picked up a Bible (I was learning that this was a pretty regular prop in these parts):

> And this man, Rowe, by his own admission . . . was a silver merchant. He worked for pay. You have read your Bible, you are church going folks, I don't have to quote the Bible to you; but I would like to refresh your memory. The one story is to be found in the Twenty-sixth Chapter of Saint Matthew, the Fourteenth through the Sixteenth Verses; and with your kind indulgence, I would like to quote it for you. It says, "Then one of the twelve, called Judas Iscariot, went unto the chief priests, and said unto them, What will you give me, and I will deliver him unto you? And they covenanted for thirty pieces of silver. And from that day on he sought opportunity to betray him."

Such a man, Hanes argued, cannot be believed. He was paid only "on the basis of information delivered; if he delivered no information, there was no pay." Without citing any evidence whatsoever, Hanes claimed that when Rowe had no information, "he would agitate and egg and urge to maybe create some trouble, and then he could go sell it."

Hanes concluded by suggesting that it was the civil rights movement that stood to gain the most from this death. That it counted on controversy, injury, and death to fill its treasury and to further its cause, adding that "No one denies Mrs. Liuzzo was slain. It was a terrible thing."

> But I submit to you . . . that her murderers are not in this courtroom, not at this table or anywhere in this court room. I don't know where they are; I wish I

knew. But I suspect that they are somewhere laughing at the poor simple people of Alabama for what fools they made out and looking for their next victim. . . . The only testimony [is] from Gary Thomas Rowe. Search your hearts, search your consciences; I know you will do what is right. Thank you.

Finally came U.S. Attorney Ben Hardeman, a longtime Montgomery lawyer, gray haired and sprightly. He spoke to the jury plainly and effectively in the familiar, homespun accents of Alabama. He would like, he said, "to help us get this train on the track, so to speak." He started with a down-home definition of conspiracy that everyone could understand:

> What are we trying in this case, anyway? We are not trying a murder case, although there was a murder in it; we are not trying the ku klux klan, or whatever the name of it is, although there are klansmen in it; we are trying three men by name, whose names appear in the indictment, on a charge of conspiracy, which in common parlance means they were in cahoots, and they were in cahoots to deprive citizens of rights that are either protected or guaranteed by the United States Government, among them being rights that were protected and declared by an order of this very court in which we are now, in reference to the very march and the very highway on which this unfortunate incident took place. In a nutshell, that is what we are trying.

Hardeman then reviewed all the evidence that corroborated Rowe's story and argued that it was absolutely conclusive. While the defense might not like it, everything that Rowe said happened on the road had been fully corroborated from other independent sources. He closed by talking to Alabamians about the threat of the Alabama klan:

> Now this case is important. It is very important. It is the most important thing in the world right now to these three men . . . but it has more importance than that. This case transcends many of the other issues that are presented. . . . Are we going to permit in the Middle District of Alabama a return to the medieval system of trial by torture? Are we going to permit a star chamber court, by persons unknown at times and places unknown, who are their own investiga-

tors, their own witnesses, their own judge, their own jury, and yes, their own executioner? Are we going to have a government of law or men? We take the flat position that all of these matters should be settled within the halls of a temple of justice such as this one. And I believe that if you consider this evidence fairly and impartially . . . you will return a verdict of guilty.

Judge Johnson then instructed the jury on the applicable law, explaining the complex legal concepts bearing on the issue to be tried. In a courtroom, this frequently tends to become a tedious and technical exercise. In the state trials, Judge Thagard had read his instructions quickly, in a soporific monotone. But somehow, when Judge Johnson said them, the words literally sprang to life. His own interest in the legal standard governing the trial was obvious, and it commanded attention. Johnson sat forward in his chair, leaned toward the jury, set his notes to the side, locked his eyes on the jurors, and explained the law in such serious tones that he seemed to saying: "You had best listen carefully. **This is the law.** It is important and you must understand it."

In his instruction the judge made clear that everyone involved must set aside thoughts of which party wins or loses. The views of the Southern Christian Leadership Conference and the united klans of America are not on trial: "So we are not concerned with the political or sociological causes in the case; we are not concerned with whether the verdict impedes their causes or whether it assists their causes." The judge went on to explain conspiracy law and related the definition to the facts of this case in the same clear and simple, but important, manner. I joined the bar in 1957 and this was by far the most impressive judicial performance I ever witnessed, before or since. The jurors seemed as spellbound as the courtroom full of spectators. As they filed out to deliberate, their somber facial expressions seemed to acknowledge that they understood and had accepted the great significance of their really tough task.

Deliberations began at 10:03 a.m. on December 2, 1965 and continued throughout the day. Twenty-four hours later they asked to see the judge and the foreman announced, "Your honor, we find that we are unable to reach a verdict and seem to be hopelessly deadlocked." In the same manner as he had delivered the instructions, Judge Johnson asked them to continue to deliberate. He pointed out that they had heard between forty and fifty witnesses and had fifty exhibits to consider, adding, "So you haven't commenced to deliberate the case long enough to reach the conclusion that you are hopelessly deadlocked."

The judge then delivered the *Allen* charge, a special legal instruction named for the first case in which the Supreme Court described it, encouraging juries to reach a verdict.[7] Courthouse regulars have nicknamed it and its successors the "dynamite charge." That charge advises that this trial has been long and expensive, that there is no reason to think the case could be tried "better or more exhaustively than it has been on either side." No juror should give up "his conscientious convictions," but you should vote according to the laws and the evidence and "not a mere acquiescence" in the conclusions of others. Judge Johnson directed that "[i]n conferring together you ought to pay proper respect to each other's opinions, with a disposition to be convinced by each other's arguments." If most of the jurors are for conviction, "a dissenting juror should consider whether a doubt in his own mind is a reasonable one which makes no impression upon the minds of so many equally honest" people who have heard the same evidence. Conversely, if the majority is for acquittal, the minority ought "seriously to ask themselves whether they ought not to consider the correctness of a judgment" reached by the others.

In delivering the "dynamite charge," Judge Johnson once again communicated directly with each juror. At one point he even rearranged their seating so he could eyeball each and every one: "Will you get six on the row, please; this lamp bothers me with the juror on the end." And, again, every juror paid close attention to every word.

At 2:08 p.m. that day, the jury returned with a verdict. The defendants had indeed been in "cahoots." Each of them was "guilty as charged in the indictments." Judge Johnson thanked the jurors for their service and stated, "if

---

7   Allen v. United States, 164 U.S. 492 (1896). Note, this was decided in the very same year as Plessy v. Ferguson, 163 U.S. 537 (1896), in which the Court had approved the separate but equal doctrine at the end of Reconstruction.

it is worth anything to you, in my opinion that was the only verdict that you could possibly reach in this case." Before pronouncing sentence, he asked each defendant if he had any statement to make. Wilkins and Eaton said only that they were "innocent of the charge." Thomas declined to make a statement. They were all sentenced to the maximum of ten years in federal prison (Roy Reed, "3 Men Get 10 Years," *New York Times*, December 4, 1965, 1).[8]

December 3, 1965, thus became the first time in modern American history that an Alabama jury had convicted klansmen for a killing in a civil rights case.[9] This first conviction by a southern jury was the product of a determined judge, a group of lawyers committed to proving the truth, and of honest jurors who had finally awakened in the twentieth century. We now see prosecutions all across the county for police misconduct such as that suffered by Rodney King in California in 1991. And we see southern police and prosecutors succeeding in old civil rights cases from Birmingham, Alabama, and Jackson, Mississippi.

The Liuzzo case changed life in America. It applied the inspirational slogan of the Holocaust survivors as our country's message to the "knights" of the ku klux klan: "never again."

---

8 The conviction would be upheld on appeal. Wilkins and Thomas v. United States, 376 F.2d 552 (5th Cir. 1967).

9 There was also progress in Anniston, Alabama, where a day earlier a white man was convicted of manslaughter for the racial motivated killing of a black foundry worker. As Taylor Branch explains, "After twenty ballots, an all-white jury convicted Hubert Strange on December 2 for the random murder of Willie Brewster on the way home from a July 1965 white supremacy rally at which [klan leaders] Connie Lynch and J.B. Stoner praised the Liuzzo ambush as a model execution." Taylor Branch, *At Canaan's Edge: America in the King Years, 1965–68* (New York: Simon and Schuster, 2006), 391.

Chapter 12

SELMA'S AFTERMATH

The first jury verdict finding klansmen guilty of violent interference with civil rights demonstrators occurred on December 3, 1965, in federal court in Montgomery, Alabama. In the fifty years since then, our country has gone through many expansive changes. Federal legislation now protects civil rights across the board, banning discrimination on the basis of race, religion, national origin, gender, age, and disability. The Supreme Court has also weighed in ruling that the fundamental right to marry extends to same-sex couples (Obergefell v. Hodges, 576 U.S. _____ (2015). In addition Congress has authorized the Attorney General to seek injunctions against local police departments engaged in "patterns and practices of discrimination."

In March 2015, my namesake son and I decided to drive to Selma to see the changes and to hear President Barack Obama's fiftieth anniversary speech about Bloody Sunday.[1] It would be twenty-five years since I spoke at the twenty-fifth anniversary march to the Alabama capitol building led by the Reverend Jesse Jackson.[2] Things have changed a lot in the fifty years since the Marchers first headed for Montgomery from their headquarters at Brown Chapel AME Church.[3]

After years of delay, the freedom movement has taken hold in numerous ways. In Selma it blossomed from convicting klansmen of violent acts

---

[1] James C. Turner, a retired public interest lawyer, is my "go to" guy on civil rights and civil liberties issues. Jim's help, comments, and insights on this book have been invaluable.

[2] My remarks on that occasion appear in the appendix, and photo 21 shows me with the Reverend Jesse Jackson.

[3] Photo 6 shows the memorial there to Dr. King, Rev. James Reeb, Viola Liuzzo, and Jimmy Lee Jackson.

against blacks, to extensive voter registration, voting, and serving in local offices. But over the years, Selma's population has decreased from 28,400 in 1960, about half black, to an estimated 19,814 in 2014, of whom about three-quarters were black. A 2014 Census estimate was that over 40 percent of Selma's blacks, twice the Alabama average, lived in poverty. When blacks began to be elected to run Selma, quarrels about school desegregation developed and white residents began moving out. Many businesses in downtown Selma have closed, leaving rental or sale signage in the withering center of town. As blacks registered to vote and began winning elections, most of Selma's white residents just packed up and moved elsewhere.

There have been other changes, too. Across from the Dallas County office building, the federal Post Office no longer has the Civil Rights Division as a tenant. Instead, that space is now the office of black Congresswoman Terri Sewall, and one can enter only with a scheduled appointment.[4] The county building has the same offices, but Sheriff Clark is now long gone.[5] Most of the employees are African American; they quickly invited us into the building, saying entrance was free for anyone, including roamers from right off the street.

The final "change" we noted in Selma was down by the Pettus Bridge. In an old building there, the federal government operates a souvenir shop and offers for sale Bloody Sunday maps, caps, T-shirts, pictures, books, and doodads. For ten bucks I got a blue baseball cap displaying a profile of the marchers with over-under labels "SELMA TO MONTGOMERY" and "NATIONAL HISTORIC TRAIL 1965–2015." (As you read this, my cap has been worn so proudly and so often that its last days, like those of its owner, may be close.)

The next morning, President Obama was introduced by March leader John Lewis, now a thirty-year Congressman from Georgia. Lewis suffered a concussion from a police baton on Bloody Sunday from Alabama officers

---

4   Notwithstanding the oral pedigree I tendered, the young black guard politely declined to allow us in to walk around the Division's old office "for old times' sake."

5   Clark was voted out of office in 1966 and died on June 4, 1997 (Margaret Fox, "Jim Clark, Sheriff Who Enforced Segregation, Dies at 84," New York Times, June 7, 2007, A33).

under orders to stop the March to Montgomery.[6] I had questioned Lewis before a federal grand jury in 1965, but despite our hardest work, it proved impossible to persuade the required twelve of twenty-three predominantly white, male grand jurors to issue indictments against police officers for their actions on Bloody Sunday.[7]

Congressman Lewis turned up the emotions of 40,000 guests by proclaiming there is "still work to be done" to "redeem the soul of America." The President stated that "John Lewis is one of my heroes," and then summarized his role on Bloody Sunday:

> And then, his knapsack stocked with an apple, a toothbrush, and a book on government—all you need for a night behind bars—John Lewis led them out of the church on a mission to change America.

The President went on to describe how the violence in Selma fifty years ago had changed our world, stressing the "imperative of citizenship" that motivated three people who "loved this country so much that they'd risk everything to realize its promise." He told of a twenty-six-year-old deacon, Jimmie Lee Jackson, killed by Alabama state police; of a Unitarian minister, James Reeb, beaten to death in Selma on March 11, 1965; and a young mother of five, Viola Liuzzo, who had driven from Detroit to try to help Dr. King, but was shot to death as the march ended.

---

6   See photos 1 and 2.

7   Under 18 USC § 242, they could have indicted the Alabama police officers, who were in uniform and quite clearly acting under "color of law," with violating the federal civil rights of demonstrators peacefully marching to the state capital to seek voting rights. But for various reasons, this jury could not quite muster the twelve votes needed to charge Sheriff Jim Clark, State Police Director Al Lingo, or any of the beaters—all those gas-masked state troopers and deputy sheriffs on horseback who were shown on national television mercilessly beating and gassing the demonstrators. Some jurors explained that the jumble of people in our photos made it too hard to identify exactly which masked police officers struck which demonstrators. But other jurors seemed even more turned off by the just-published news accounts about the ongoing black rioting in Watts, 2,500 miles away in California. Somehow those actions were translated into declining to charge white violence in Alabama. It still smarts and rankles that in this, my very first federal grand jury presentation, we failed to get a single indictment for the outrages committed on Bloody Sunday.

Of these heroic deaths, the president said: "That's what it means to believe in America. That's what it means when we say America is exceptional." And, he concluded, that fifty years after Selma and 239 after our nation was found-ed, "[O]ur union is not yet perfect, but we're getting closer. . . . Somebody already got us through that first mile. Somebody got us over that bridge.[8]

With the 1965 jury convictions in the *Liuzzo* case, civil rights prosecu-tions began to fall into place across the South. In 1966, the U.S. Supreme Court's *Price* decision reversed the dismissals of the federal conspiracy cases in Mississippi and Georgia brought under 18 USC § 241. In 1967, John Doar, now an experienced and successful federal prosecutor, obtained convictions in the so-called Mississippi Burning case against the klansmen who in 1964 had murdered civil rights workers Michael Schwerner, Andrew Goodman, and James Chaney. In 1968, Dr. King and Bob Kennedy were assassinated, blacks rioted everywhere, the Poor People's Campaign camped on the Na-tional Mall, the Fair Housing Act passed, and stronger sentences were au-thorized for civil rights crimes. Under Title VII of the 1964 Civil Rights Act, police departments nationwide had to recruit from all branches of the population. In the streets, with the death of Dr. King civil rights faded in prominence and demonstrations focused more and more on ending the war in Vietnam.

And, gradually, by 1977, the Civil Rights Division could report regu-lar successes in its criminal prosecution program across the entire nation, obtaining convictions in over 67 percent of its cases, some far beyond the South. Starting with the *Liuzzo* conviction in 1965, the Division expanded its use of the Reconstruction civil rights laws, and state prosecutors, with no statute of limitations on the cold racial death cases sleeping in their files, be-gan to dig them out and take another look. The results have been gratifying.

Consider just two states of the Deep South, Mississippi and Alabama, where, after decades of frustration, some measure of justice has finally been served in heinous klan murders.

---

8   President Obama and Congressman Lewis then led thousands across the Pettus Bridge, see photo 22.

Mississippi

+ In 1994, thirty-one years after his crime, and after two mistrials, klansman Byron De La Beckwith was convicted of the murder of Medgar Evers, and was sentenced to life imprisonment, dying in prison in 2001.
+ In 1998, thirty-two years after his crime, klan imperial wizard Samuel Bowers was convicted of killing Vernon Dahmer of the Hattiesburg NAACP.
+ In 2005, forty-one full years after helping to kill civil rights workers Michael Schwerner, Andrew Goodman, and James Chaney in Neshoba County, Edgar Ray Killen, 80, was convicted of manslaughter.

Alabama

+ In 2010, forty-five years after he shot and killed Jimmie Lee Jackson of Marion, an act which led to Bloody Sunday in Selma, a guilty plea to manslaughter was entered by former state trooper James Bonard Fowler.
+ On September 15, 1963, four young black girls were killed in the bombing of the Sixteenth Avenue Baptist Church in Birmingham. After fourteen years, klansman Robert Chambliss was convicted of murder in 1977; after twenty-nine years klansman Thomas Edwin Blanton Jr. was convicted in 2001; and, almost forty years after the crime, klansman Bobby Frank Cherry was convicted in 2002.

The federal government also now has in place a new program to review all "cold" cases, many involving klan suspects. In 2008, Congress passed the Emmett Till Unresolved Civil Rights Crime Act of 2007 with an annual appropriation of $10 million for the Justice Department to "investigate all unresolved civil rights murders" that occurred before 1970.[9] On December 16, 2016, President Obama signed a new law (S2854, 114th Congress) ex-

---

9   Pub. L. 110–344, Oct. 7, 2008, 122 Stat. 3934.

tending that Act through 2027 and expanding the coverage period of such cases through the 1970s.[10]

Whenever I am asked to choose the most important case I ever worked on, I always begin with that very first one, the federal conspiracy case against the murderers of Viola Liuzzo. In retrospect, we can now see that it was the beginning of the end of excusing illegal klan terrorism and heralded the birth of a brand-new tradition of equal justice under the law.

---

10 The Justice Department has brought two successful civil rights death prosecutions, one before the Till Act (United States v. Avants, 367 F.2d 433 [5th Cir. 2004]) and one after its passage (United States v. Seale, 600 F.2d 973 [5th Cir. 2010]). Defendants in each case were sentenced to life in prison. Under the Till Act, the Department reviewed 113 civil rights matters involving 126 deaths, and referred eight matters to state authorities for possible prosecution. In addition the Department explains that in "53 . . . cases closed without prosecution, all identified subjects were deceased," and that in another "32 of the closed cases there was insufficient evidence of a potential violation of a criminal civil rights statute, as opposed to an accidental death, a suicide, a heart attack" (Attorney General's Sixth Annual Report to Congress Pursuant to the Emmett Till Unresolved Civil Rights Crime Act of 2007, May 2015, 3-4, 6).

EPILOGUE

According to the ancient Chinese proverb, a journey of a thousand miles begins with a single step.

—JOHN F. KENNEDY, ADDRESS ON THE NUCLEAR TEST BAN
TREATY, JULY 26, 1963

The Klan Defendants appealed their convictions to the Fifth Circuit Court of Appeals. The convictions were affirmed (376 F.2d 552 [5th Cir. 1967]) and the United States Supreme Court declined further review. William Eaton, who had a heart condition, died during the appeal. Both Collie Wilkins and Eugene Thomas completed their prison terms and were released in about seven years. Both are now dead. In 1966 Thomas was also tried by Alabama for the murder of Viola Liuzzo in Hayneville before a jury of eight blacks and four whites drawn under a new jury selection plan ordered by the federal court. Rowe did not testify, the prosecution relied on ballistics evidence only, and the defense offered the previously rejected alibi. This state jury acquitted Thomas.

The Supreme Court ruled in 1966 that the Civil Rights Division indictments of klansmen in Mississippi and Georgia were improperly dismissed and remanded the cases for trial, United States v. Price, 383 U.S. 787 (1966). In November 1967, in a federal court in Jackson, Mississippi, Assistant Attorney General John Doar and lead prosecutor Deputy Assistant Attorney General Bob Owen, backed by a support team from the Civil Rights Division, obtained civil rights convictions of Deputy Sheriff Cecil Price and six codefendants for the killings of civil rights workers Michael Schwerner, Andrew Goodman, and James Chaney (the Mississippi Burning case). This was the first conviction of white police officials and klansmen in Mississippi for federal crimes against civil rights workers and blacks.

Lowndes County, Alabama totally revamped its jury system in 1966 pursuant to a federal court order in a case litigated by the ACLU and Civil Rights Division attorneys and Research Analysts. The court ruled that under the Constitution every citizen including all women and blacks must be included in jury pools and fairly considered for jury service. The Lowndes County voter registration drive continued to encourage blacks to register with the federal examiners, producing a black registration majority of over 60 percent. All Lowndes County elected officials are now black.

Stokely Carmichael (Kwame Ture), who led the Lowndes County voter registration drive, died of prostate cancer in Conakry, Guinea, in November 1998, at age fifty-seven.

Gary Thomas Rowe lived a very eventful life after these trials but never changed his account of the Liuzzo murder. After the trial, he temporarily changed his name to Thomas Neil Moore and entered the federal witness protection program. On May 25, 1998, at sixty-four years old, he was found dead of an apparent heart attack in Savannah, Georgia. After Rowe testified in the three Liuzzo trials covered in this book, the FBI provided him with a lump-sum payment to compensate him for his informant work and arranged a federal law enforcement job for him in California.[1] Unable to succeed in this new work, Rowe returned to Georgia.

Divorced and now out of funds, Rowe claimed that the FBI owed him more than he had been paid, but his claim was rejected. In 1975, wearing a hood to conceal his appearance, he provided details about his five years as an FBI informant to the U.S. Senate Select Committee to Study Governmental Operations with Respect to Intelligence Activities (the Church Committee).[2] During Rowe's days as an informant, the FBI's management of informants was very informal (see Gary May, *The Informant: The FBI, the Ku Klux Klan, and the Murder of Viola Liuzzo* [New Haven: Yale University Press, 2005]). Based in part on Rowe's testimony, the 1976 report of the Church Committee caused Attorney General Ed Levi to issue detailed

---

1   Under the new Guidelines adopted by Attorney General Edward Levi, payment of informants is now regulated much more strictly.

2   He appears in a mask in photo 20.

departmental rules (the Levi Guidelines) governing use of informants and gathering intelligence. Following the Church Committee recommendations, the rules governing informants have now been strengthened significantly. Since issued, these guidelines have been updated and amended regularly.

In 1976, with help from a ghost writer, he published a biographical book, Gary Thomas Rowe, *My Undercover Years in the Ku Klux Klan* (New York: Bantam Books, 1976). In 1979, after Eugene Thomas had served his conspiracy sentence, he testified before an Alabama grand jury that it was Rowe, not Wilkins, who had fired the fatal first shots at Mrs. Liuzzo. That grand jury voted an indictment, but, after a full hearing, the State of Georgia declined to extradite Rowe to Alabama and the charge was dropped. In 1982, in a federal civil suit for damages filed by the Liuzzo family, a federal judge declined to credit the claims by Thomas that Rowe had killed Viola Liuzzo and dismissed the case. John Doar and I testified as government witnesses in that trial.

Arthur C. Gamble Jr. became circuit judge after the retirement of Judge Thagard (deceased February 8, 1975). Gamble died at age eighty-eight on July 17, 2008. He was seriously injured in the early 1970s when his car was bombed by a man he had convicted. His surviving wife, Bobbie, lives in a retirement home in Greenville, Alabama.

Richmond Flowers died on August 9, 2007. He was defeated in his 1966 campaign for governor by George Wallace's wife, Lurleen. Along with his assistant, Joe Breck Gantt, Flowers was indicted and convicted in 1969 of charges brought by the U.S. attorney in Birmingham. The jury found that they violated the Hobbs Act by committing or conspiring to commit extortion while Flowers was attorney general. Flowers was sentenced to eight years in prison. United States v. Flowers, 448 F.2d 815 (5th Cir. 1971). After exhausting all appeals, he began serving his sentence in 1972 and was released after eighteen months. He received a pardon in 1978 from President Carter. He also cooperated in a biography written by John Hayman, *Bitter Harvest: Richmond Flowers and the Civil Rights Revolution* (Montgomery: Black Belt, 1996), with an introduction by former President Carter. The book's very serious accuracy issues are discussed in chapter 10, p. 76, note 6.

George Corley Wallace was an unsuccessful candidate for President in 1968 and 1972. He was shot in 1972 while campaigning in Maryland and spent the rest of his life in a wheelchair. After his wife's death he successfully ran twice more for Governor of Alabama. In his last campaign in 1982, he renounced his segregationist past, and was elected with the support of most of the state's black voters. Wallace died in 1998. In the week after his death, Congressman John Lewis wrote in the *New York Times* ("Forgiving George Wallace," September 16, 1998) that Wallace had sought "redemption for his mistakes" and "acknowledged his bigotry" and "I had to forgive him, because to do otherwise . . . would only perpetuate the evil system we sought to destroy." He closed by saying that forgiveness "serves a higher moral purpose" and that "[t]hrough genuine repentance and forgiveness, the soul of our nation is redeemed."

Leroy Moton spent several years working for SCLC in the mid-1960s. He is now retired and presently lives in Hartford, Connecticut. He and the author continue to be friends.

The united klans of America has been in a steady decline. In 1981 some of its members lynched Michael Donald, a black man, near Mobile, Alabama, and were convicted in Alabama state courts of murder. One of them was sentenced to death. The Southern Poverty Law Center in Montgomery, founded by attorney Morris Dees, filed a federal civil suit on behalf of the deceased victim's family. In 1987, a jury in Mobile awarded them a judgment of seven million dollars and, to satisfy it, the black family was given title of the klan's only remaining asset, a small office building, which became that family's residence. (See Jesse Kornbluh, "The Woman Who Beat The Klan," *New York Times Magazine*, November 1, 1987.)

Frank M. Johnson continued to serve on the federal district court bench in Montgomery through the 1970s. He required Alabama to reapportion its legislative and congressional districts, and found gross violations of the Constitution in the conditions in State prisons and mental health facilities. In 1977 President Carter nominated him to be Director of the FBI, but the judge withdrew for health reasons. In 1979, he was elevated to the federal appeals court. In 1992, the Federal Courthouse in Montgomery was named in his honor. He died in 1999.

John Doar died on November 11, 2014. He left the Civil Rights Division in 1967 and practiced law in New York City. In 1973 and 1974 he served as Impeachment Counsel for the House Judiciary Committee considering the impeachment of President Richard Nixon.

The Liuzzo family became convinced over the years that the FBI had been negligent in supervising Tommy Rowe and should pay the family damages for her death. In 1979, the family filed suit against the Bureau in federal court in Michigan. After a full evidentiary hearing in 1983, the case was dismissed by the judge. The victim's husband, Anthony James Liuzzo, died in 1978. Two books were written about the victim's life and death: Mary Stanton, *From Selma to Sorrow: The Life and Death of Viola Liuzzo* (Athens: University of Georgia Press, 1998), and Beatrice Siegel, *Murder on the Highway: The Viola Liuzzo Story* (New York: Four Winds Press, 1993). In 2006, a documentary, *Home of the Brave*, was made about the Liuzzo family by Paola di Florio.

Selma, Alabama was the scene in 1989 of the swearing in of three black county commissioners, giving blacks control of the Dallas County Commission. Gerald Jones, chief of the Voting Section, Civil Rights Division, and the author, as Acting Assistant Attorney General, attended this swearing in. In September 2000, after thirty-six years in office, Mayor Joe Smitherman was defeated by black candidate James Perkins Jr.

The author was named in 1969 to serve as the career Deputy Assistant Attorney General of the Civil Rights Division, a post he held continuously until May 1994. He served the Department in nine national administrations for seventeen Attorneys General. He was cited in 1983 as a Distinguished Executive by President Reagan. He writes about civil rights from his home in Maryland. Publications include his autobiography, *The Other Side of the Mountain*.

APPENDIX

Remarks of James P. Turner
Acting Assistant Attorney General,
Civil Rights Division, United States Department of Justice
Montgomery, Alabama March 10, 1990

On behalf of President Bush and Attorney General Thornburgh, I commend the SCLC and the organizers of this event. More personally, as one whose professional life was energized twenty-five years ago by the events we celebrate today, I thank you for the rare honor and privilege of participating in this celebration. As you heard in the introduction, I have been continuously in the business of enforcing civil rights laws since the days twenty-five years ago when I was sent here by the Justice Department to conduct a grand jury investigation of the events of Bloody Sunday and to serve on the team of federal prosecutors that finally brought to justice the klansmen who murdered Viola Liuzzo—a Detroit woman who was gunned down on Route 80 after the Selma march.

In 1965, black people in this state lived at the lowest level of a pervasive caste system—invisible to the law and unacceptable to society. The Civil Rights Movement—the idea whose time had come—eliminated that system forever.

Within months of the Montgomery March, President Johnson signed the Voting Rights Act, the strongest civil rights bill ever conceived in this country. In Alabama alone, black registration increased from about 92,000 in 1964 to nearly a quarter of a million in 1967. Nationwide, the number of black elected officials has leaped from 103 in 1964 to 7,226 today. In Alabama, there were no black elected officials in either the Alabama House or the Alabama Senate at the time of the Voting Rights Act. Today, there are five black state senators and eighteen black House members. After the census counts in 1970 and 1980, hundreds of units of state and local government across the South were reconstituted, but on these occasions the Voting Rights Act required that every single plan be inspected for racial fairness by the Justice Department's Civil Rights Division. For example, we found that one congressional district in Atlanta was drawn to minimize the chance that a black congressman could be elected. We required the lines to be drawn fairly and in 1972 that district elected Andrew Young and today it is served by none other than John Lewis—whom I first met as one of the leaders of the Bloody Sunday March.

And, under other provisions of the Act, unfair voting systems may now be challenged in federal court. For example, we are today completing a trial in Los Angeles, California, where we contend that a county of seven million people has been divided purposefully into five election districts in a way that fragments two million Hispanic residents to prevent their representation. In Selma, where it all began, after ten years of contested litigation, the Department of Justice was finally able to get a fair districting plan in place, and just last year I had the honor of attending the swearing-in of three new black members of the five-person Dallas County Commission—a swearing-in conducted by Alabama's first black federal district Judge, U. W. Clemon.

So I want to join with you today in celebrating the monumental events which led to these historic changes in American life. They happened, of course, because of the exercise of the rejuvenating right to petition for redress of grievances contained in our Constitution and enforced by our courts. The rights of all Americans were enhanced when the Marchers crossed the Pettus Bridge to expose the oppression of Selma and begin a quest for justice in Montgomery and beyond. But such events also happened because of the inspired vision of Dr. King and the others who literally devoted their lives to exercising the power of freedom. In one of his finest moments, Dr. King stood in this historic spot in March of 1965 and declared to the world:

They told us we wouldn't get here. And there were those who said that we would only get here over their dead bodies. But all the world today knows that we are here, that we are standing before the forces of power in the state of Alabama, saying "We ain't goin' let nobody turn us around."

And, that is truly a story that deserves the telling, and the retelling, lest anyone forget that it is the miracle of freedom that its power grows strongest when it is threatened most.

The cause of racial justice was pushed—firmly but peacefully. The tactics were as straightforward as a simple plea for fairness: truth was preached in the churches; oppression was demonstrated in the streets; justice was practiced in the courts. And with a grace that was truly amazing, an entire nation peacefully healed itself.

I like to think that the spirit of the Montgomery March is the true spirit of democracy, that the ideas unleashed twenty-five years ago here in Alabama surfaced again in Tiananmen Square; that the march of ideas that started here are now reverberating in Johannesburg and Prague; and that the first cracks in the Berlin Wall had their seismic origins in Selma, Alabama, in 1965.

But such claims are perhaps too grandiose. Let me settle for the thought that the events we celebrate today should inspire all of us to have a higher faith in America.

For my part, I renew to you my personal promise, and the firm commitment of the Justice Department, that the civil rights laws of this great country will be vigorously enforced. To ensure that the precious gains of black voters are not lost in post-1990 redistricting, we will faithfully review every new district formed after next month's national census to ensure full compliance with the Voting Rights Act. With the FBI, we will relentlessly search for the killers of Judge Vance and civil rights attorney Robert E. Robinson. We will bring those responsible to justice.

Today, we join together not so much to celebrate the successful completion of a chapter of national life, as to renew the overarching commitment to equal justice under law. We know that this goal has yet to be realized, but I hope that each of us leaves here with a revitalized determination to continue to work for the dream of justice and racial understanding envisioned by the Marchers from Selma.

Thank you.

INDEX OF CASES, NAMES, AND REFERENCES